I0504657

Scrum for Hardware Explained

Achieving Industrial Agility

Paolo Sammicheli

Scrum for Hardware Explained

Achieving Industrial Agility

Paolo Sammicheli

ISBN 9798397938815

Leanpub

This is a Leanpub book. Leanpub empowers authors and publishers with the Lean Publishing process. Lean Publishing is the act of publishing an in-progress ebook using lightweight tools and many iterations to get reader feedback, pivot until you have the right book and build traction once you do.

This work is licensed under a Creative Commons Attribution-ShareAlike 4.0 International License

Contents

Appendix 199

This page intentionally left blank

Dedication

To my friend Paolo "Peo" Gozzi, who left us way too early.

Peo, we miss you so much.

Acknowledgements

This book would not have been possible without the hundreds of people I have had the honor of coaching on the various teams described in this book. This book showcases the methods and practices of people who have found better ways to work. But behind each professional journey are the human stories of dedicated individuals who put their hearts into challenges and accomplished more than what they ever thought possible.

Thank you! The heroes are you, not me coaching you.

Thanks to all my colleagues and friends who supported and encouraged me. A hug and infinite thanks go to Joe Justice for his unconditional support and friendship. I also thank and hug Andrea Provaglio and Deborah Ghisolfi for the continuous intellectual exchange that makes us grow together. I also am deeply grateful to Jeff Sutherland and all the wonderful people at Scrum Inc. for their support and help.

A huge thanks to Fabio "Pixel" Colinelli, who, for the second time, drew the cover of my book[1].

I would also like to thank those unknown people who left rough reviews of my first book. You people made a major contribution to tickling my ego and encouraging me to write a better book. I hope you will now find what you wanted to know and had not found in "Scrum for Hardware."

If you still find missing information upon completing this book, please let me know by writing to me via my website or directly on social media.

Paolo Sammicheli - https://paolo.sammiche.li

---

[1]You can read an interview with Fabio and learn more about him on the Scrum-AI website: https://www.scrum-ai.com/blog/the-design-on-the-cover-is-awesome-who-s-the-artist

Foreword

When I think of Paolo, I think of his visits to my home in Sweden along with our mutual friend Joe Justice. In addition to fine Italian wine, he always brings interesting stories and anecdotes from his journey with Scrum in hardware. The visits usually end with a lake swim despite frigid winter temperatures. Paolo is the only one of us smart enough to resist the peer pressure and watches with amusement as we engage in this form of ritual self-torture (although it does feel nice afterward, but I'm not sure he believes us).

Anyway, about the book you are about to read: Congratulations! You made a good choice :)

I often get the question - "Does Scrum work in Hardware"? This is a fair question since the Scrum framework was born in a software context, and most books and examples of Scrum are based on software. My short answer is "Yes." Scrum is a framework for dealing with complex problem-solving in almost any domain. But you need to adapt the practices, and the devil is in the details.

That's what I appreciate about Paolo's book. He manages to strike a perfect balance between theory and practice. What's better than fluffy hand-wavy theories? Fluffy hand-wavy theories backed by concrete, real-life examples! The book is full of references to research papers, articles, models, and patterns. But it also backs those up with practice - real-life stories and photos from Scrum in hardware and other non-software contexts. The practical examples provide hands-on tips and tricks, while the theory explains the 'why' behind the 'how,' which is crucial for adapting the practices to your context.

Now, when I get that question, I'll simply point to Paolo's books (yes, this is his second book on the topic).

Paolo is too humble to admit it, but this book is actually broader than just Scrum in hardware. I would recommend it to anyone trying to figure out how to apply Scrum in a broader context than just software.

Hope you enjoy it!

And we'll see if we manage to get Paolo to hop into the cold water sometime...

/Henrik Kniberg

Paolo Sammicheli, Riccardo Mariti, Joe Justice, and Henrik Kniberg.

Why another book on Scrum and Hardware

As the Author
I want to explain why I'm writing a new book on Scrum for Hardware
So that people might understand whether they want to read it.

You may wonder, why another book on Scrum and Hardware? As the author of the first significant publication in the world on the topic, I feel it important to address this question upfront. This book's structure, fresh insights, and new material are the answer. Unlike my first book, which shared stories chronologically, in the order I learned them, this one follows the progression of an organizational transformation. This structure likely aligns better with your journey as a reader, providing guidance and insights exactly when you need them. Two years have passed since the second edition, and the world of Scrum on hardware has evolved. This book includes new material reflecting those changes and developments, ensuring you're up-to-date with the current landscape. Additionally, I've incorporated knowledge I developed while writing my recent book on Artificial Intelligence. I have refined and improved the content based on valuable feedback and my own increased experience.

I hope this book will be a comprehensive guide for anyone embarking or continuing on their Agile journey, no matter their starting point. Enjoy the read!

Paolo Sammicheli

Open-Source Agile Publication

In the journey of learning how to write a book, inspired by the Agile Movement and the Open Source community, I came to these principles that will lead the writing of my books:

1) Free as in Freedom

Unless otherwise specified, the publication is distributed under the Creative Commons BY-SA[2] license. This gives the freedom to copy, share and show in public this material with any media and create derivate work for any purpose, even commercially, under the following terms:

- **Attribution** — You must give appropriate credit, provide a link to the license, and indicate if changes were made. You may do so reasonably but not in any way that suggests the licensor endorses you or your use.
- **ShareAlike** — If you remix, transform, or build upon the material, you must distribute your contributions under the same license as the original.
- **No additional restrictions** — You may not apply legal terms or technological measures that legally restrict others from doing anything the license permits.

---

[2]https://creativecommons.org/licenses/by-sa/3.0/

2) On the shoulder of giants

This publication will not reinvent the wheel, wasting your time presenting somebody else's ideas in different words to avoid plagiarism. When another publication is considered exhaustive on a specific topic will be quoted and linked, leaving the reader to decide whether to invest time in learning more from the source. Sources available with the same permissive license will be preferred over restricted material.

3) Early and Continuous delivery of valuable content

The highest priority is to delight the readers through early and continuous delivery of fresh, valuable content. We will try to do that frequently. We will simplify the new content's navigation with a Hyper Textual Change Log at the beginning of the publication.

4) Ultimate Edition

Multiple editions will be published, adding new stories and practices to be discovered with clients every time. Readers who buy the book from any source will get free access to the electronic version, continually updated on Leanpub[3]. Nobody will need to pay for future editions, and everybody will receive all the updates forever. It's a promise!

Sharing my work with the **Open-Source Agile Publication principles** is the best way I know to create a better world and give thanks to the giants who came before us.

---

[3]https://leanpub.com/scrum-hardware-explained/

How to get the updates

You can download the electronic version on Leanpub.com for free by going to the end of the book and using the QR Codes provided. You will also get a free QR Code to download the previous book "Scrum for Hardware."

Due to some restrictions following the GDPR law, Leanpub is not automatically subscribing new users to the updates' mailing list. So, to be sure to be notified every time there's a new version available (don't worry, it will be one email per month or less), go to your Leanpub account, "Library" -> "Books." Then, select the book and mark "New Version Available" under Email Settings.

How to subscribe to updates notification

Introducing myself

As the Author
I want to introduce myself
So that the readers know the context from where I learned this book's material.

My name is Paolo Sammicheli, Sammy to my friends. I was born in Siena - Italy, a charming town in Southern Tuscany, famous for its Palio[4], an ancient horse race held twice a year. I am a computer scientist. Technology has always been my passion. I was eleven when I first tried to program a computer. It was my Commodore 64, an absolute novelty for those times and a luxury. It had just arrived from faraway America, and it cost nearly one million Italian Liras, around 500€ today, but given the cost of living at that time was a real asset for a kid like me. We were pioneers in the early eighties: we programmed in BASIC, and software was loaded using 5¼-inch floppy disks or cassette tapes. I soon realized that this was what I wanted to do in my life, and, at nineteen years old, Information Technology became my profession.

I got my diploma in Computer Science from the Industrial School in 1991, and I immediately started working in IT Firms.

As a teenager, I volunteered for many years, driving ambulances for the Misericordia di Siena[5], a 750-year-old welfare organization, and also taking part in humanitarian expeditions in Italy and abroad with the Civil Protection Group. When, in the late 1990s, I discovered the Free Software[6], it was love at first sight. All those programs developed by volunteers, which you could legally copy, study and

---

[4]https://en.wikipedia.org/wiki/Palio_di_Siena
[5]http://www.misericordiadisiena.it
[6]https://en.wikipedia.org/wiki/Free_software

modify, represented a technology plus volunteering combination that I sensed remarkably close to my vision of the world. I was among the most active members of the Siena Linux User Group[7]. My friends were there too, and we organized conferences and events to raise awareness of free software in schools, universities, and sometimes even town squares.

The free operating system spreading rapidly in the 2000s was Ubuntu[8]. In the Bantu language, spoken in Central Africa, Ubuntu means "humanity towards others" or "I am what I am because of who we all are." Building a better computer system, accessible and free for everybody was the vision of the project's founder, the South African entrepreneur Mark Shuttleworth[9]. I joined the project in 2006, and thanks to my volunteering, I quickly earned the Italian community's esteem and friendship. Towards the end of 2007, I mainly dealt with translation and marketing. I founded the **Italian Ubuntu Marketing Team**. I had set the goal of organizing in-person gatherings for the community members who usually had online contacts only.

When, in 2008, I started contributing to the international community and traveling every year to the US to attend the Ubuntu Developer Summit, I was employed by an Italian Software company as the Technical Director of the central Italy branch.

Thanks to the Ubuntu International community, I first glanced at how an Agile Organization would look. From the technical point of view, the organization was impressive: we had 3000 remote contributors worldwide, developing, testing, and releasing software with automated tests and continuous integration daily. The operating system's stable version had a release cycle of six months, less than one-quarter of any other commercial operative system. From a cultural point of view, the community was an incredibly welcoming and collaborative environment. The morale was exceptionally high,

---

[7]http://siena.linux.it
[8]https://www.ubuntu.com
[9]https://en.wikipedia.org/wiki/Mark_Shuttleworth

and even though there were highly talented people, the ego was usually low. I fell in love with Agility and started applying to the company I was employed in, even though the culture was not so welcoming and the results were very different. I didn't give up and enrolled in a Certified Scrum Master and a Product Owner class to learn more.

From 2008 I experienced this double professional life, with fun and stellar productivity in Ubuntu and frustration and unproductivity in my daily job. Finally, in 2014, I resigned because I was not too fond of my employer's politics. I started my career change, founding my own company with Alessandro, an ex-colleague that left the company just after me.

My company was supposed to be mainly a Software Firm, offering Agile coaching and training as a complementary business. In the same year, Agile became very popular in Italy, so client after client, I worked as a full-time Agile Business Coach and left my company's software development side to Alessandro. To me, that meant moving from Silicon to Carbon, in other words, from working with computers to people.

In 2016 I had the opportunity to implement Scrum with Hardware in an Industrial context. I met Joe Justice, a Scrum Trainer founder of the Wikispeed project[10], and other pioneers in learning more about Scrum applied to Hardware development. This experience allowed me to speak about this topic in a TEDx[11]. Since then, Joe and I have become close friends, and I have been lucky enough to co-train with him multiple times in the US and Europe and visit clients. In 2017 I transformed my diary of these fantastic experiences with him into my first book: Scrum for Hardware[12]. The fate was nice to me: this book has been recognized as the first significant publication in the world on the topic and received considerable exposition in the US, Europe, and Japan.

---

[10]https://en.wikipedia.org/wiki/Wikispeed
[11]http://scrum-hardware.com/tedxsiena-paolo-sammicheli/
[12]https://leanpub.com/Scrum-for-Hardware

My book's success led me to meet and co-train with Jeff Sutherland[13], co-author of Scrum, the Agile Manifesto, and founder of
Scrum Inc[14]. After some training together, Jeff asked me if I was
interested in becoming a licensed trainer for his company. My
career took a boost: as a Scrum Inc's Scrum Trainer, I taught and
coached Scrum Teams in successful companies in a wide range of
industries: Machinery, Construction, Oil&Gas, IoT, Pharmaceutical,
Banking, Food, Beverages, Aeronautics, and Aerospace.

In 2019, I got interested in Artificial Intelligence thanks to a random
beer with a former GoogleX Engineer who was spending his
holidays in Tuscany. The same year, AI's interest increased among
my clients, and they started developing Artificial Intelligence applications.

In March 2020, during the first Italian lockdown due to the Covid-
19 Pandemic, I took advantage of the lonely weekends at home
to enroll in an online Artificial Intelligence course at MIT Sloan,
where I learned a lot and met incredibly talented people.

These learnings ignited my interest in AI. Following this first course,
I enrolled in other more technical online courses and started playing
with models on my computer and the cloud. We were at the first
lockdown that extended to almost every country. Many of my
clients organized online happy hours to socialize together, and the
topic of my sharing was my learnings about AI. So, some clients
asked me to coach their AI teams. That year I had the opportunity
to coach AI teams working on Machine Learning in Financial and
NLP in Pharma. I started collecting experiences and practices, and
the following year, I started writing my second book: Scrum in AI -
Artificial Intelligence Agile Development with Scrum and MLOps[15].
The book came out in electronic version on June 18th, 2021, featured
with the foreword by Jeff Sutherland. From that moment, during
the rest of 2021 and 2022, I interviewed multiple teams developing

---

[13]https://en.wikipedia.org/wiki/Jeff_Sutherland
[14]https://www.scruminc.com
[15]https://www.scrum-ai.com

AI, which led to the release of the paper version on Amazon before Christmas 2022.

In the second half of 2022, I began to travel again to coach Hardware teams. The sales of my book about hardware started to grow, and the topic became more interesting for a larger audience. At the beginning of 2023, I realized that my second book structure was better than my first one, and I had a lot of interesting material in the AI book that would also apply to Hardware.

So, here we are. I decided to write this third book about Hardware as a mashup of more recent material and with the same structure as my AI book. I hope you will find it helpful to help you achieve Industrial Agility in your company. At the end of this book, you'll find the free coupon to download my first book, "Scrum for Hardware," for free, hoping that this will complement your understanding of Agile Hardware Development.

Fundamentals

As the Author
I want to recap the fundamentals
So that anybody can enjoy this book regardless of experience level.

Is this first part for you?

In this part, I'll recap Agility's basic notions, which are not explicitly related to Hardware development. Seasoned Agile practitioners would be tempted to skip this first part. From a certain point of view, they might be right. I recommend browsing these chapters anyway, especially the Scrum Pattern chapters. I often found this topic to be unknown to most Agile practitioners. Scrum Inc. teaches the Scrum Patterns starting from the two-day Scrum Master class, typically considered entry-level training. Having co-trained with Jeff Sutherland multiple times, I feel this material to be part of the basics. Other Scrum certification bodies and respected trainers do not teach the Scrum Patterns, and many consider them optional or just for seasoned coaches. So, don't miss it because I'll mention them during the second part, explicitly covering Hardware development without explaining what a Pattern is.

Agile

As the Author
I want to introduce the topic of Agile
So that the reader can understand the real meaning of
Agile without the hype associated with it.

What means Agile? The commonly used definition comes from the **Agile Manifesto**, described later in this chapter:

Responding to Change over Following a Plan

Nevertheless, before showing the 2001 Agile Manifesto, I would like to start talking about the more recent definition of Agile I know from Alistair Cockburn[16]:

"Agile is the ability to move and change direction, quickly and with ease."

The Heart of Agile

Alistair Cockburn is one of the 17 authors of the **Agile Manifesto**, and he recently published "The Heart of Agile[17]."

---

[16]https://en.wikipedia.org/wiki/Alistair_Cockburn
[17]https://heartofagile.com

The Heart of Agile

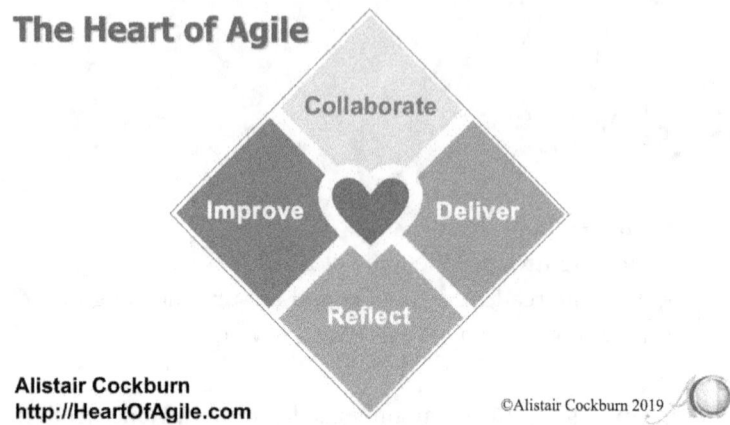

Alistair Cockburn
http://HeartOfAgile.com

©Alistair Cockburn 2019

His idea of agility has been synthesized in 4 words: Collaborate, Deliver, Reflect, and Improve. The logo is a visual tool that allows people to reflect and brainstorm what these words mean in our context. Alistair provides a set of concepts and tools for each one of the four keywords. By expanding the concept from the center to the exterior, tools can become broader and more extensive.

The Heart expands into Details

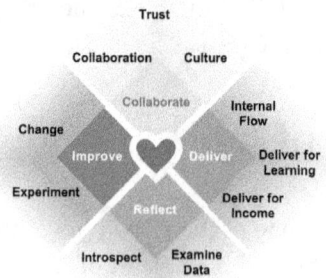

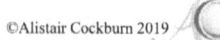
©Alistair Cockburn 2019

Deliver

Internal flow

Any organization in the world could be described as a giant brain where there are people making decisions. Everything delivered is an embodiment of decisions, and findings build upon other choices. This internal flow of decisions needs to be visualized and improved to make the organization improve.

From this point of view, anything we deliver is made of Decisions. Alistair's research shows that an error is made in every 5-10 decisions. How do we deal with this, then? Alistair says that by making decisions visible with visual management tools, we can improve this flow of decisions with the same principles of Lean Manufacturing[18]. With these practices, we can remove waste and optimize the flow.

Deliver for learning

Whenever an organization delivers something, feedback happens. Agility uses feedback to build a loop that constantly leads to improvements. The slight improvement, known as Kaizen in the Japanese tradition, allows for systemic advancement thanks to the constancy. Agile methods like Scrum allow significant changes thanks to frequent replans, known in Japanese as "Kaikaku." Combining intelligently "Kaizen" and "Kaikaku" leads to getting ahead of the competition in organizational learning and getting a competitive advantage.

Deliver for income

Delivery is always associated with an exchange of value. Frequent deliveries produce a regular return on investments. The reduction

---

[18]https://en.wikipedia.org/wiki/Lean_manufacturing

of the ROI timing reduces risks and enables the company to provide greater agility.

Reflect

Examine data

This topic includes the behavioral aspects of stopping and inspecting the data and the good habits of collecting and rationalizing data to get insight. Effective use of AI consists of these needs, combined with the big data technologies needed to manage an exponentially growing set of information.

Introspect

Stopping and checking data also includes checking emotions. We're human beings, and we can only perform if we're comfortable with ourselves. To explore this topic, I suggest looking for literacy about Retrospectives, especially the book Agile Retrospectives[19] by Diana Larsen and Ester Derby.

Improve

Change

In his training, Alistair suggests "Solution Focus" as an approach for this manner. What is the Solution Focus? The solution-focused brief therapy approach[20] grew from the work of American social workers Steve de Shazer[21], Insoo Kim Berg[22], and their team at the Milwaukee Brief Family Therapy Center (BFTC) in Milwaukee, Wisconsin.

I found a good description of it in the coachingleaders.co.uk[23]

---

[19]https://www.goodreads.com/book/show/721338.Agile_Retrospectives
[20]https://en.wikipedia.org/wiki/Solution-focused_brief_therapy
[21]https://en.wikipedia.org/wiki/Steve_de_Shazer
[22]https://en.wikipedia.org/wiki/Insoo_Kim_Berg
[23]https://coachingleaders.co.uk/what-is-solution-focus/

website:

> Solution Focus is a big idea that focuses on small steps and keeping them simple. This means that you can start using it to improve your business and your life straight away. (...) Although it originated as a therapy model, the Solution Focus approach is now successfully applied to coaching and team and organizational change.

Solution Focus is based on 4 Principles:

- Focus on solutions, not problems
- People already have the resources they need to change
- Change happens in small steps
- Work at the surface level

Even though it is possible to read books to understand the method, attending a workshop would be advised. With an in-person seminar, it would be easier to learn how to use the technique with individuals and teams.

Experiment

Every time you improve something, that is because you change it. But not every change will be an improvement. So, the best way is to proceed with changing stuff with small experiments. For this topic, I personally recommend PopcornFlow by Claudio Perrone. It's a system of continuous experimentation that I found very useful, especially in complex problems. You can find more information about it in the Appendix, where I interviewed the author.

Collaborate

Collaboration and Communication

The ability to communicate and collaborate effectively is vital to have a functional work environment. In his workshop, Alistair teaches multiple techniques to improve collaboration, primarily based on visualization and enabling everybody to express themselves.

Culture and Trust

A team is not a group of people working together. It's a group of people who trust each other[24].
Culture could be defined as a set of Values and Beliefs shared in an organization. Whether it is being cultivated or not, organizational culture exists and drives the decisions not regulated, made in a discretional way. Often, only 20% of the decisions at work are driven by specific rules and norms. 80% of the decisions are driven by values and a set of shared beliefs. Cultivating the Company Culture is vital if we want most of the findings to align with the organization's strategy.

An excellent example of how an organization can develop and nurture its culture is the Zappos case study. I highly recommend the book Delivering Happiness[25] by the late Tony Hsieh[26], an easy-to-read and incredibly inspiring book, also available as an audiobook read by the author.

---

[24]Quote by Simon Sinek: https://www.osmquote.com/quote/simon-sinek-quote-5b40d4
[25]https://en.wikipedia.org/wiki/Delivering_Happiness
[26]https://en.wikipedia.org/wiki/Tony_Hsieh

The Agile Manifesto

The original Agile Manifesto[27] was created during a meeting in 2001 at Snowbird, Utah.
The 17 participants came from different backgrounds and methods: eXtreme Programming, Scrum, DSDM, and other software consultants. They come out with a set of shared values that are considered the essence of all the methods represented.

Manifesto for Agile Software Development

We are uncovering better ways of developing
software by doing it and helping others do it.
Through this work we have come to value:

Individuals and interactions over **processes and tools**

Working software over **comprehensive documentation**

Customer collaboration over **contract negotiation**

Responding to change over **following a plan**

That is, while there is value in the items on
the right, we value the items on the left more.

Principles behind the Agile Manifesto

After the meeting, the participants kept talking through emails about what the Manifesto meant in practice and published twelve principles behind it:

1. Our highest priority is to satisfy the customer through early and continuous delivery of valuable software.

---

[27]https://agilemanifesto.org

2. Welcome changing requirements, even late in development. Agile processes harness change for the customer's competitive advantage.
3. Deliver working software frequently, from a couple of weeks to a couple of months, with a preference to the shorter timescale.
4. Business people and developers must work together daily throughout the project.
5. Build projects around motivated individuals. Give them the environment and support they need, and trust them to get the job done.
6. The most efficient and effective method of conveying information to and within a development team is face-to-face conversation.
7. Working software is the primary measure of progress.
8. Agile processes promote sustainable development. The sponsors, developers, and users should be able to maintain a constant pace indefinitely.
9. Continuous attention to technical excellence and good design enhances agility.
10. Simplicity–the art of maximizing the amount of work not done–is essential.
11. The best architectures, requirements, and designs emerge from self-organizing teams.
12. At regular intervals, the team reflects on how to become more effective, then tunes and adjusts its behavior accordingly.

Today: Product, not Software

After the Manifesto was published, some authors pointed out that it wasn't really about software only but could be applied to any product. There wasn't a general consensus about rephrasing it for a more general purpose, so it remained unchanged from the first formulation. However, many Agile Manifesto authors, I have seen

Jeff Sutherland and Alistair Cockburn, override the word "software" with "product" in their presentations and course material to make the Agile Manifesto usable in a more general way.

Further readings

- Agile Software Development[28] - Alistair Cockburn
- Agile and Iterative Development: A Manager's Guide[29] - Craig Larman
- The Age of Agile[30] - Steve Denning

---

[28]https://www.goodreads.com/book/show/942577.Agile_Software_Development
[29]https://www.goodreads.com/book/show/1229810.Agile_and_Iterative_Development
[30]https://www.goodreads.com/book/show/34963438-the-age-of-agile

Scrum

As the Author
I want to introduce the topic of Scrum
So that I clarify what Scrum is and what is not

Scrum Basics

Scrum is an Agile framework designed to develop complex projects, created by Jeff Sutherland and Ken Schwaber and presented for the first time at the OOPSLA 1995 Conference[31]. Scrum and its rules are described in the Scrum Guide[32], freely available online. However, the best definition of Scrum comes from the recent update of the Scrum Guide, November 2020:

> Scrum is a lightweight framework that helps people, teams, and organizations generate value through adaptive solutions for complex problems.
>
> In a nutshell, Scrum requires a Scrum Master to foster an environment where:

- A Product Owner orders the work for a complex problem into a Product Backlog.
- The Scrum Team turns a selection of the work into an Increment of value during a Sprint.
- The Scrum Team and its stakeholders inspect the results and adjust for the next Sprint.
- Repeat

---

[31] http://www.jeffsutherland.org/oopsla/schwapub.pdf
[32] https://scrumguides.org

The Scrum Framework elements are eleven: **3 Roles, 5 Events, and 3 Artifacts**. According to the authors, any implementation lacking even just one of these cannot be called Scrum since they are meant to reinforce each other.

The 3 **Roles** of Scrum, described as "Accountabilities," are *Scrum Master*, *Product Owner*, and *Developers*. Collectively they are called the **Scrum Team**.

The Scrum Master is accountable for establishing Scrum as defined in the Scrum Guide. They do this by helping everyone understand Scrum theory and practice, both within the Scrum Team and the organization. In addition, the Scrum Master is accountable for the Scrum Team's effectiveness. They do this by enabling the Scrum Team to improve its practices within the Scrum framework. In other terms, Scrum Master's accountability is to improve the productivity of the Scrum Team.

The Product Owner is accountable for maximizing the value resulting from the Scrum Team's work. The Product Owner is also accountable for effective Product Backlog management, like creating and clearly communicating Product Backlog Items, managing stakeholders' expectations, and defining Product Backlog items' priority. The Product Owner may do the mentioned activities or may delegate the responsibility to others. Regardless, the Product Owner remains accountable.

Developers are the Scrum Team professionals committed to creating any aspect of a usable Increment for each Sprint.

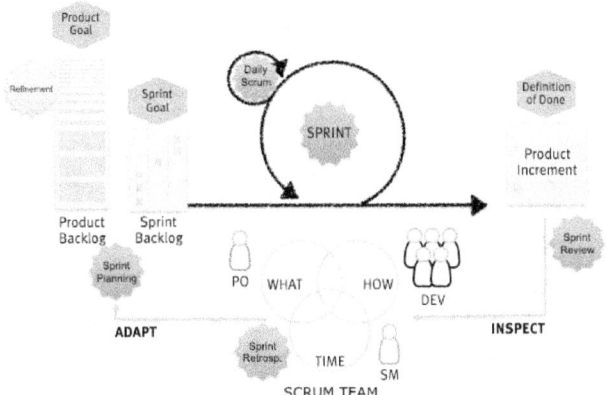

Scrum's artifacts, *Product Backlog, Sprint Backlog,* and the *Increment,* represent work or value. They are designed to maximize the transparency of essential information.

Each artifact contains a commitment to ensure it provides information that enhances transparency and focuses so that they can measure the progress:

- For the Product Backlog is the Product Goal.
- For the Sprint Backlog is the Sprint Goal.
- For the Increment, it is the Definition of Done.

These commitments exist to reinforce empiricism and the Scrum values for the Scrum Team and their stakeholders.

The Product Backlog is a list of *items* sorted by value containing the product's information to be developed. The Product Owner is solely responsible for its prioritization.

The Sprint Backlog is a list of *items* that have to be developed during the Sprint.

An Increment is a concrete step ahead toward the Product Goal. Each Increment consists of the done work performed during the

Sprint integrated with the Increments produced in the previous Sprints. To provide value, the Increment must be usable, hence compliant with the Definition of Done.

The Scrum Team works in iterations of constant duration, called Sprint; every Sprint has a maximum length of 4 weeks and acts as a container for all Scrum events. During the Sprint, the following *events* take place:

- *Sprint Planning* is the meeting at the beginning of the Sprint that lays out the work to be performed for the Sprint. This resulting plan is created by the collaborative work of the entire Scrum Team.
- *Daily Meeting* takes place every day, for no more than 15 minutes, in the same place and at the same time. During the Daily, the Developers align on the previous day's work, the work to be carried out the same day, and possible difficulties.
- *Sprint Review*, a meeting at the end of the Sprint, open to the Scrum Team and any concerned stakeholders to inspect the work produced during the Sprint to determine future adaptations.
- *Retrospective*, a meeting that takes place immediately after the Review and concluding the Sprint. The Scrum Team considers any improvements and organizes them accordingly.

Finally, the *Product Backlog Refinement* is the continuous activity where the Scrum Team creates, detail, clarify, and estimates the Product Backlog Items for the future Sprints.

A Healthy Tension

The reason why it is appropriate that three different people embody the three Scrum roles is clearly explained in the video by Henrik Kniberg "PO in a NUTSHELL[33]". In developing a product of any type, there are three objectives we want to achieve.

---

[33]https://www.youtube.com/watch?v=502ILHjX9EE

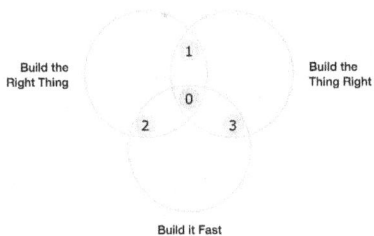

- *Build the right thing*: we want to build the right and valuable product functionality for our clients.
- *Build the thing right*: we want to build the right product from an engineering perspective.
- *Build it fast*: we want to get to the market as quickly as possible.

Ideally, everyone wants to be at point **0** of the diagram, perfectly balanced between the three elements. What happens if we find ourselves at point **1**? We built the right product, and we did it technically very well. However, we have been too slow, and our competitors have already conquered the best customers. The road is uphill, and we will hardly manage to make up for a lost time.

What happens if we find ourselves at point **2** instead? We built the right product quickly. However, our product is technically fragile, customers complain, and medium-term correction of defects and maintenance costs kill the company's profits. Certainly not a good deal. Finally, what happens if we find ourselves at point **3**? We built a beautiful cathedral in record time. Unfortunately, our clients did not want a cathedral — they just wanted a tent. So our expensive product will remain on the shelves gathering dust. Scrum's organization seeks to keep the projects close to point **0** by dividing prerogatives between the three roles.

The *Product Owner* will focus primarily on understanding what features are beneficial and more valuable; that is, "*the right thing.*" The *Developers* will focus on building the product in a technically effective way or building "*the thing right.*"

The *Scrum Master* will focus on the process, so productivity increases and reduces the feedback loop.

The faster the learning cycle, the more the Scrum Team will understand how to maintain stability near point **0**. This *Healthy Tension* is the reason for having these three distinct accountabilities.

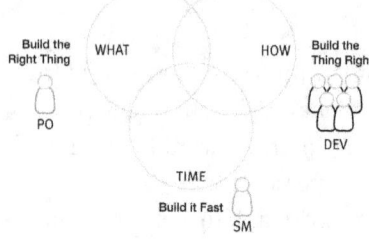

Develop competencies

Scrum requires the Scrum Team to be cross-functional. All the skills necessary to create the product reside in the team to carry out all the processing steps during the Sprint. It may be that people with specialized skills, employed in a non-continuous way during the development cycle, are under-utilized in some phases of the Sprint. To prevent this from happening and allow team self-organization, Scrum encourages the development of T-Shaped Skills in all team members. In this case, the T represents a competence matrix in which each team member has a rudimental skill in each area required by product development. At the same time, he has an advanced level of knowledge in one of the sectors.

What does it mean? Suppose we represent the various skills on a matrix. Junior implies that the person can do some developments under the guidance and the advice of a Master of that skill. Senior means that the person can develop in autonomy, and Master means the person has a deep knowledge of the topic and can teach and mentor Junior people.

In that case, we can see a T-shaped diagram, where each basic skill is placed in a corresponding area involving the product. A piece of Mastery is placed in one of them.

	Skill 1	Skill 2	Skill 3	Skill 4	Skill 5	
Junior						
Senior						
Master						

T-Shaped Skills

However, in LeSS - Large Scale Scrum, Craig Larman asserts that to obtain high-performing teams, it is necessary to create the conditions for people to develop pi-shaped skills, i.e., in the form of π (pi). Pi Skill means a solid primary skill, a secondary discrete skill, and a rudimental skill in all other aspects.

	Skill 1	Skill 2	Skill 3	Skill 4	Skill 5	
Junior						
Senior						
Master						

Pi-Shaped Skills

Larman also asserts that, in this situation, people should act as mentors in their primary skill and carry out most of the activities in the secondary skill to continue to deepen the lesser-known subject.

A Theory of Scrum Team Effectiveness

In June 2021, Jeff Sutherland sent a recent paper to us, the Scrum Trainers licensed by his company, a recent paper from Cornell University by the title "A Theory of Scrum Team Effectiveness[34]" by Christiaan Verwijs and Daniel Russo. This paper, published after a seven-year-long investigation on almost 1.200 Scrum teams, proposed and validated a theory for effective Scrum teams, focusing on internal dynamics, a topic that is rarely covered in similar research. Moreover, it results in a formalization of clear recommendations for how organizations can better support Scrum teams.

What does Team Effectiveness mean? Two main variables characterized the effectiveness of Scrum teams according to the interviewed teams:

- Stakeholder Satisfaction
- Team Morale

The findings suggest that the most effective Scrum Teams can **release frequently** (in the schema Responsiveness) and have a clear understanding of what their **stakeholders need** (Stakeholders Concern), but not one or the other. Following the picture of the theoretical model.

---

[34]https://arxiv.org/abs/2105.12439

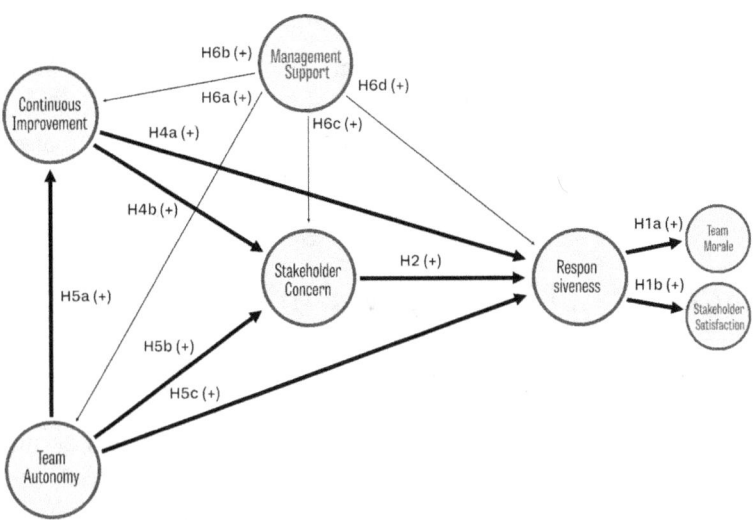

Other factors influence "Stakeholder Concern" and "Responsiveness," and those are being clusterized into Team Autonomy, Continuous Improvement, and Management Support. Then, they used the findings from the case studies and insights from extant literature to induce a theoretical model to explain how team-level factors contribute to the effectiveness of Scrum teams and formulated some hypotheses:

- Hypothesis 1 (H1). The Responsiveness of a team is positively associated with team morale (H1a) and stakeholder satisfaction (H1b).
- Hypothesis 2 (H2). Stakeholder concern is positively associated with Responsiveness
- Hypothesis 3 (H3). The positive relationship between stakeholder concern on the one hand, and team morale and stakeholder satisfaction on the other is fully mediated by Responsiveness
- Hypothesis 4 (H4). Continuous improvement is positively associated with stakeholder concern (H4a) and Responsiveness (H4b)

- Hypothesis 5 (H5). Team autonomy is positively associated with continuous improvement (H5a), stakeholder concern (H5b), and Responsiveness (H5c)
- Hypothesis 6 (H6). Management Support is positively associated with team autonomy (H6a), continuous improvement (H6b), stakeholder concern (H6c), and Responsiveness (H6d).

Summary of Findings and Implications

Five Factors Team Theory

From 13 case studies, they developed a theoretical model for Scrum teams from thirteen lower-order indicators grouped into five latent factors. This model fits the data from a large and representative sample of Scrum teams well. Furthermore, the five factors explain a substantial amount of variance in stakeholder satisfaction and team morale. As an implication, the suggestion is to design and assess Scrum teams with five team-level factors in mind: Responsiveness, stakeholder concern, continuous improvement, team autonomy, and management support. Then, create the environment of Scrum teams to minimize constraints to these factors on the one hand and train and support them in the skills they need.

Responsiveness

Responsiveness is positively associated with team morale and stakeholder satisfaction. The suggestion is to support Scrum teams in their ability to be responsive. Implement technical tooling, increase automation, and train necessary skills (particularly the Product Backlog Refinement). Invest in team autonomy, stakeholder concern, and management support to make the need for Responsiveness more relevant to teams.

Stakeholder Concern

The stakeholder concern of teams is positively associated with Responsiveness. Indirectly, stakeholder concern is also positively associated with Team Morale and stakeholder satisfaction. Nevertheless, this positive effect is only present when Responsiveness is high, i.e., fully mediated by Responsiveness. Product Owners can increase Stakeholder Concern by co-opting teams in product strategy formulation, goal setting, and collaboration with stakeholders. If Scrum teams are unable to release frequently in the first place, efforts must be undertaken to remove organizational constraints, increase automation and build technical skills.

Continuous Improvement

The degree to which teams engage in continuous improvement is positively associated with stakeholder concern. Contrary to our expectations, continuous improvement is not significantly associated with Responsiveness. Scrum teams are advised to direct their continuous improvement process towards the five critical factors identified in this study: Responsiveness, stakeholder concern, team autonomy, management support, and continuous improvement. These factors are most likely to highlight constraints to team effectiveness stemming from internal or external factors to the team. In turn, organizations should broaden the autonomy of teams to encourage them to take control over improvements.

Team Autonomy

Team Autonomy was positively associated with continuous improvement and stakeholder concern. Therefore, the recommendation is to expand the autonomy of Scrum Teams primarily in two areas. The first is internal to teams and concerns the degree to which its members are cross-functional. The second concerns constraints imposed by the organizational environment that limit control over tooling, team composition, choice of process, and Product Owners' mandate over their product.

Management Support

Management Support was found to be positively associated with team autonomy, continuous improvement, and stakeholder concern, but no significant effect was found on Responsiveness. Management can most effectively contribute to Scrum teams by increasing their autonomy, both in self-management and product mandate. Train management in the skills needed to support rather than direct.

Areas of the Factors

Each factor described in the Theoretical Model, except the Management Factor, are exploded in primary areas:

- Stakeholder Concern
    - Value Focus
    - Stakeholder collaboration
    - Sprint Review Quality
    - Shared Goals
- Team Autonomy
    - Self-Management
    - Cross Functionality
- Continuous Improvement
    - Sprint Retrospective Quality
    - Quality Concern
    - Psychological Safety
    - Shared Learning
- Responsiveness
    - Release Frequency
    - Refinement

The relationship between them and the associated data are depicted in the following picture.

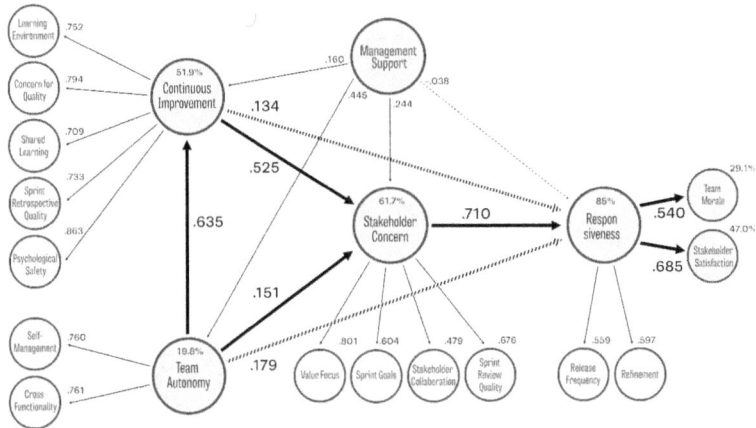

Standardized factor loadings and standardized path coefficients for the research model. All paths, except dotted lines, are significant.

Further readings

- Scrum: The Art of Doing Twice the Work in Half the Time[35] - Jeff Sutherland
- The Scrum Fieldbook: A Master Class on Accelerating Performance, Getting Results, and Defining the Future[36] - JJ Sutherland
- Software in 30 Days: How Agile Managers Beat the Odds, Delight Their Customers, And Leave Competitors In the Dust[37] - Jeff Sutherland, Ken Schwaber
- A Theory of Scrum Team Effectiveness[38] - Christiaan Verwijs and Daniel Russo

---

[35]https://www.goodreads.com/book/show/19288230-scrum
[36]https://www.goodreads.com/book/show/43582738-the-scrum-fieldbook
[37]https://www.goodreads.com/book/show/13589272-software-in-30-days
[38]https://arxiv.org/abs/2105.12439

Scrum Patterns

As the Author
I want to introduce the topic of the Scrum Patterns
So that the reader understands how to make high-performing teams and to design effective organizations.

Scrum Patterns

In software engineering, the concept of *design pattern* can be defined as "a general design solution to a recurring problem." It is a description, or a logical model, applied for resolving a problem that may frequently occur, even before defining the computational part's solving algorithm. It is often a practical approach to contain or reduce technical debt.[39]

Patterns' concept came from Architecture and originated by Christopher Alexander[40], a widely influential British-American architect and design theorist currently emeritus professor at the University of California, Berkeley. His theories about the nature of human-centered design have affected fields beyond architecture, including urban design, software, sociology, and others.

In the late Nineties, The Pattern Language became popular in the Software community. The first Scrum patterns were published in 1997 in a Paper by Mike Beedle, together with Devos, Sharon, Schwaber, and Sutherland, with the title SCRUM: An extension pattern language for hyperproductive software development[41]. The

---

[39]Adaptation of the definition of a Design Pattern from Wikipedia: https://en.wikipedia.org/wiki/Design_pattern
[40]https://en.wikipedia.org/wiki/Christopher_Alexander
[41]http://jeffsutherland.org/scrum/scrum_plop.pdf

first Agile Patterns book "Organizational Patterns of Agile Software Development[42]" was published in 2005 by Jim Coplien and Neil Harrison.

Since 2010 the ScrumPlop[43] community meets annually to collect, catalog, and publish the patterns that performing teams around the world adopt using Scrum.

ScrumPloP Nyteboda, Sweden. 16-19 May 2010

Neil Harrison, Mike Beedle, Jim Coplien, Jeff Sutherland

In 2019, thanks to the work of the ScrumPlop community facilitated by Jim Coplien, who served as a Product Owner, a second book was published, with the title "A Scrum Book: The Spirit of the Game[44]" by Jim Coplien, Jeff Sutherland and the Scrum Plop community.

How to Read a Pattern

The structure of a Pattern is meant to simplify the browsing of the publication. Rarely the Patterns books are intended to be read from cover to cover. More frequently are used as reference when in need of a specific source of inspiration. Following a schema of a Pattern's structure.

---

[42]https://www.goodreads.com/book/show/756250.Organizational_Patterns_of_Agile_Software_Development

[43]http://www.scrumplop.org

[44]https://www.goodreads.com/book/show/45029885-a-scrum-book

Structure of a Pattern

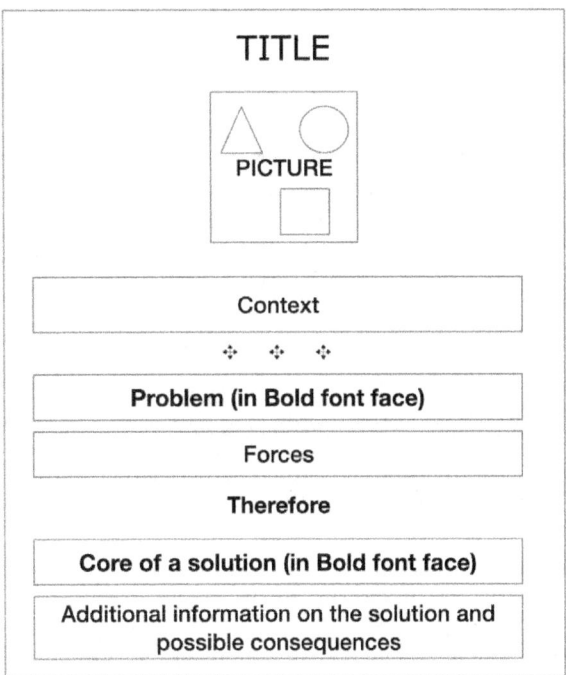

The pattern always has a title and a picture associated. This serves as a way to enable visual memory. Then there's a description of the context and the reference of dependencies from other Patterns. The typographic symbol separates the context from the **Problem** statement in bold font face. Further information of the forces that this problem creates follows, and then the word **Therefore** leads to the core of the **Solution**, still in bold. Underneath the core of the solution, there is detailed information, with examples, images, possible consequences, and a list of sources.

Teams that Finish Early Accelerate Faster

In 2013 Jeff Sutherland presented at Agile Alliance 2013 in Nashville[45] a talk about nine of what he consider the most useful Scrum Patterns.

He proposed this collection as the first fundamental element to create a High Performing Team. It's the Scrum Inc. recommended starting point for a Scrum Master, just after implementing the Scrum Guide elements properly. The list of the patterns is the following:

- Stable Teams
- Yesterday's Weather
- Swarming: One-Piece Continuous Flow
- Interrupt Pattern: Illegitimus Non-Interruptus
- Daily Clean Code
- Emergency Procedure
- Scrumming the Scrum
- Happiness Metric
- Teams that Finish Early Accelerate Faster

While the Scrum Guide[46] provides basic Scrum rules, patterns amplify it by showing how teams can solve problems in particular contexts. According to the Scrum authors, Scrum should be simple, fast, and fun. For many new Scrum Masters, Scrum is difficult, slow, and painful instead. Performance patterns are designed to remedy the various headaches encountered by the Scrum Masters in coaching teams' activity.

---

[45]https://www.agilealliance.org/resources/sessions/coaching-simple-patterns-that-avoid-common-pitfalls-for-scrum-teams/

[46]http://scrumguides.org

Stable Teams

This pattern suggests keeping the teams stable, avoiding moving people continuously from one Team to another. Stable Teams tend to agree and learn more about their skills, making estimates more reliable and allowing the business to be predictable. In traditional organizations, workgroups often change when the project changes; in Agile organizations, the work flows towards stable teams, not vice versa.

Yesterday's Weather

In many cases, the amount of Product Backlog Items completed during the previous Sprint is the best indicator of the amount of PBIs completed in the following Sprint. With this pattern, the Team plans Sprint items based on the last three sprints' average. When the Team achieves everything before the end of the Sprint, another ready Product Backlog Item will be *pulled* from the Product Backlog in agreement with the PO.

Swarming: One-Piece Continuous Flow

When a team is struggling to complete the Sprint work, the cause may be that too many things started simultaneously (*work in progress*). This happens if the Team is not focused on finishing first the most valuable item. *Swarming* together on one thing to complete it quickly increases the performance of the entire Sprint. How does it work? Whoever takes charge of the highest priority item is considered the "captain" of the Team. Everyone has to help him, and nobody should interrupt him. As soon as the captain finishes the first item, anyone taking the following item is the new captain.

Interrupt Pattern: Illegitimus Non-Interruptus

This pattern allows the allocation of a time buffer for any unplanned work and prevents it from exceeding. It is based on three simple rules that will enable the company to organize itself to avoid losing the production rhythm:

1. The Team creates a buffer for interruptions based on historical data. For example, if it turns out that 30% of a team's work comes from unplanned work, with a velocity of 60 points, 20 are reserved for the interruption buffer.
2. All requests must go through the Product Owner. It will be considered whether to insert them in the Product Backlog to do them in the following sprints, reject them entirely, or insert them into the current Sprint interruption buffer. The Team starts working on the new activity only after completing the current one.
3. If the buffer exceeds the maximum size, the Product Owner calls the "Sprint Abort" procedure and notifies the management that release dates may slip.

This last rule means that the buffer does not exceed except in extreme circumstances. If used in conjunction with Yesterday's Weather pattern, its size gradually levels to the minimum possible. A reducing buffer increases the Sprint capacity accordingly and allows the Team to accelerate.

Daily Clean Code

The correction of problems by the same day they have detected aims to get a flawless project and reduce maintenance costs. It is already known in Lean practices that immediate correction of root problems improves production capacity.

Emergency Procedure

When the burn-down chart does not show progress towards the Sprint Goal, we suggest this procedure. It is similar to the one used for a long time by the pilots of airplanes.

When a problem emerges, immediately execute the specific emergency procedure without understanding what does not work. It is the responsibility of the Scrum Master to ensure that the procedure is carried out directly, preferably within half of the Sprint. Here are some steps of the emergency procedure. Use the necessary ones:

1. Change the way the work is done. Do something differently.
2. Ask for help, usually by transferring some of the work to someone else.
3. Reduce the Sprint scope.
4. Abort the Sprint and plan again.
5. Inform the management of any impact on the release dates.

Scrumming the Scrum

Identify the single most crucial impediment and remove it within the next Sprint. The impediment removal item is placed in the Sprint Backlog as a higher-priority user story. It is provided with acceptance criteria that determine when it is completed. Then evaluate the state of the story during the Sprint Review along with the others. This pattern was part of the Sprint Retrospective description in the 2017 version of the Scrum Guide[47] and removed again in the 2020 version to simplify the framework.

---

[47]http://scrumguides.org

Sprint Backlog: Day X

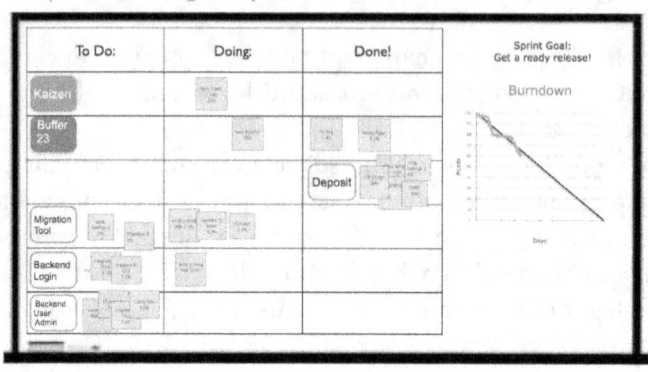

scruminc.

Scrum Board example, by ScrumInc

Happiness Metric

Happiness is one of the best metrics because it is a predictive indicator. When people think about how happy they are, they are projecting how they feel in the future. If they believe that the company is in trouble or doing something wrong, they will feel sad. If there are any impediments or a frustrating rule system, they will feel sad. A compelling way to understand the status of a team is to know how happy they are. The Scrum Master asks two questions:

- How happy are you about the company?
- How happy are you about your role?

Team members answer questions on a scale of 1 to 5. These numbers are kept in a spreadsheet and tracked weekly. If the numbers change significantly, it is essential to talk with the Team to find ways to make them happier. By monitoring the Team's morale, the Scrum Master successfully anticipates the drops in velocity and acts proactively.

Teams that Finish Early Accelerate Faster

Teams often accept an excessive workload in the Sprint and cannot finish it. Recognizing failure and being always under pressure are elements that prevent the Team from improving. Therefore, it is advisable to take less work, maximizing the chances of success, using, for example, the Yesterday's Weather pattern. Then, the other Patterns of the list that reduce the Sprint impediments must be implemented, allowing for managing the interruptions and finishing the Sprint Backlog in advance. When the Developers complete the work in advance, it can take the most valuable item from the backlog. This will ensure that the value of Yesterday's Weather grows in the following sprints. To increase the probability of accelerating, it is good to apply Scrumming the Scrum to identify the retrospective's improvement activities and place it as the top priority in the next Sprint.

Further readings

- ScrumPlop[48] Website
- A Scrum Book[49] - free online version
- A Scrum Book: The Spirit of the Game[50] - Jeff Sutherland, James O. Coplien, and The Scrum Patterns Group
- Organizational Patterns of Agile Software Development[51] - James O. Coplien, Neil B. Harrison

---

[48]http://www.scrumplop.org
[49]http://scrumbook.org/
[50]https://www.goodreads.com/book/show/45029885-a-scrum-book
[51]https://www.goodreads.com/book/show/756250.Organizational_Patterns_of_Agile_Software_Development

In Practice

As the Author
I want to detail the method, composed of specific practices useful in Hardware development
So that this book will help people to achieve Industrial Agility.

This chapter collects the patterns and practices to implement Agile and Scrum in the Industrial Manufacturing context effectively. If you do not clearly understand the basics, I recommend reading the previous part, The Fundamentals.

Industrial Agility

As the Author
I want to introduce the topic of Industrial Agility
So that readers understand why to embark on this journey.

The Quest for Speed

In today's global economy, time-to-market has become the ultimate competitive weapon. With the advent of the Fourth Industrial Revolution[52], we're witnessing an unprecedented surge in technological advancements, accelerating the pace of change. Klaus Schwab[53], founder of the World Economic Forum[54], defined the Fourth Industrial Revolution as the following:

> "In the new world, it is not the big fish which eats the small fish, it's the fast fish which eats the slow fish."

This metaphor aptly sums up the current business environment. As companies grapple with rapid changes in consumer behavior, technology, and market trends, speed, and adaptability become critical survival skills. The same sentiment is reflected in a famous old quote by former General Electric CEO Jack Welch[55], who warns:

> "If the rate of change on the outside exceeds the rate of change on the inside, the end is near."

---

[52]https://en.wikipedia.org/wiki/Fourth_Industrial_Revolution
[53]https://en.wikipedia.org/wiki/Klaus_Schwab
[54]https://www.weforum.org
[55]https://en.wikipedia.org/wiki/Jack_Welch

On the automotive, this sentiment is reinforced by Volkmar Denner[56], the CEO of the Bosch Group, who underscores agility as a critical success factor:

> "For Bosch, agility is crucial; it allows us to adjust to the increasing speed of change around us."

Herbert Diess[57], Volkswagen Group CEO:

> "Volkswagen risks ending up like Nokia, the giant that used to dominate the cell phone market and then lost the challenge of switching to smartphones. The big question is: Are we fast enough? If we continue at our current speed, it is going to be very tough."

The Diess' concerns were about the switch to electric cars; a market dominated at the moment of writing by Tesla. Elon Musk[58], Tesla's CEO, often repeats:

> "Pace of innovation is all that matters in the long run."

What does it mean for Business?

In terms of business, this means more than just keeping up with the pace of change; it requires a fundamental shift in how companies are designed and operate. Organizations must adopt an operating system that promotes responsiveness, quick decision-making, and continual learning. It's about streamlining processes, eliminating waste, and creating an environment where innovation thrives.

---

[56]https://en.wikipedia.org/wiki/Volkmar_Denner
[57]https://en.wikipedia.org/wiki/Herbert_Diess
[58]https://en.wikipedia.org/wiki/Elon_Musk

This transformation isn't limited to software development or tech companies. It's equally applicable to the industrial and manufacturing sector, where an agile approach can result in more efficient production processes, higher quality products, faster response times to market changes, and, ultimately, a more competitive and resilient business.

Why Hardware Must Embrace Agile Principles

Steve Denning[59], in his June 2020 Forbes article "Why Hardware Must Embrace Agile Principles[60]" presented a compelling argument that the slower pace of innovation in hardware, as compared to software, is not solely due to heavier regulation, but also because how hardware manufacturing is managed in large firms and their inattention to the customer's needs.

Denning points out that the manufacturing process is often designed to be slow. For example, a significant redesign in a product, such as a car door, can take years because of the financial investment in the equipment necessary for production. However, Denning argues, "With modern techniques, such as 3-D printing and general-purpose robots, it's possible to make rapid changes at relatively low cost." The main barrier is the management's unwillingness to do anything about the sunk cost of manufacturing equipment and process changes.

Denning also criticizes the prevalent mindset within hardware companies that dictates traditional manufacturing methods, limiting flexibility and responsiveness to changing customer needs. This mindset is the opposite of the Agile principles, focusing on

---

[59]https://en.wikipedia.org/wiki/Steven_Denning
[60]https://www.forbes.com/sites/stevedenning/2020/06/21/why-hardware-must-embrace-agile-principles/

modularity, constant iteration and feedback, and aversion to high-cost, hard-to-change systems.

He notes that firms like Tesla and SpaceX now apply Agile principles to hardware manufacturing. This approach enables rapid, iterative design changes and constant testing. The shift from traditional manufacturing also disrupts the existing supply chain infrastructure, as illustrated in the transition to electric vehicles, which have fewer components and require fewer suppliers.

On a broader note, Denning underscores the need for a different kind of leadership for this transition to happen. He suggests leaders should be more product-focused, like Elon Musk, rather than concentrating on financials and market performance. Also, he believes there's a need for a 'software-first' mentality, especially when considering new opportunities enabled by global, instant, near-zero-cost connectivity.

He gives examples of companies like Tesla, SpaceX, Volvo Cars, and Haier, which are successfully adopting these changes, as opposed to older manufacturing companies whose focus on shareholder value and bureaucracy has often resulted in a decline in innovation and value creation.

In conclusion, Denning argues for a shift in the principles of hardware manufacturing towards a customer-focused, flexible, and innovative approach, in line with Agile principles. He believes that hardware companies can improve their innovation and value creation by adopting the principles and mindset that have proven successful in software development.

Characteristics of an Agile Organization

An Agile Organization differentiates itself by its distinct traits of adaptability, responsiveness, and an ongoing commitment to learning and development.

Adaptability, the first essential characteristic, is the ability of an Agile company to adjust its strategies, operations, products, and services to suit a dynamic business environment. This capability allows them to rapidly react to and capitalize on emerging market trends and shifting customer preferences. Instead of viewing changes as threats, Agile companies consider them opportunities for innovation and growth.

Secondly, an Agile Organization values responsiveness. Responsiveness, in the Agile context, is more than just speed. It's about making rapid, informed decisions to maintain a competitive edge. This approach encourages businesses to become proactively involved in market changes and to act swiftly to meet new challenges head-on. Responsiveness in this context also entails quickly delivering high-quality products or services to the market, keeping pace with or surpassing competitors.

Furthermore, an Agile Organization is characterized by a commitment to continual learning. It encourages an organizational culture where learning is an ongoing process, not a one-time event. This continual learning involves regularly acquiring new skills, embracing new technologies, and refining business models based on market feedback and trends. By fostering a culture of constant learning, Agile companies can adapt to change more quickly and maintain a significant edge over less agile competitors.

An Agile company precedes individuals and their interactions over rigid processes and tools. It places its employees - their skills, talents, creativity, and collaboration ability - at the heart of its operations.

Moreover, Agile companies seek to build a cooperative relationship with customers beyond simple business transactions. By engaging customers in the development process, Agile companies can better understand their needs and desires, creating more effective solutions.

The cornerstone of an Agile Organization is its ability to respond to change over a stubborn adherence to following a plan. Sticking to a set plan can hinder growth and innovation in a dynamic business environment. Agile companies, therefore, consider their plans to be flexible and adapt them as needed in response to changing market conditions.

In an Agile organization, teams are not just simple work groups. They are cross-functional, comprising diverse, motivated individuals with various skills and expertise. This diversity promotes creative problem-solving and innovation. They are self-organizing, meaning they have the authority to manage their own work and make critical decisions. This autonomy encourages a sense of ownership and accountability, leading to higher productivity and job satisfaction.

These Agile teams work in short, focused iterations or sprints. Each iteration aims to deliver incremental value to the customer. This iterative approach allows for faster feedback, quicker detection of errors, and more timely improvements.

Finally, Agile companies are committed to continuous improvement. They understand that customer feedback and changing requirements are not hindrances but catalysts for improvement. They continuously strive to enhance their products, services, and processes based on the invaluable insights gathered from customer feedback and market changes. Thus, they evolve, keeping them resilient and competitive in an ever-changing business landscape.

Is it only about Agility?

While agility is a crucial component, the transformation doesn't stop there. It's also about digital transformation - leveraging modern technologies like artificial intelligence, the Internet of Things, and cloud computing to gain productivity, faster feedback, and rapid innovation.

Digital transformation enables businesses to gather and analyze data in real-time, providing invaluable insights to drive decision-making and innovation. Artificial intelligence can automate routine tasks, enhance product quality, and optimize resource utilization.

In manufacturing, digital transformation means smart factories where machines and systems can communicate and cooperate with each other and humans in real-time. It's about Industry 4.0, where cyber-physical systems, automation, and the Internet of Things converge to create a more interconnected and efficient manufacturing environment.

In conclusion, Industrial Agility is not just about being fast; it's about being smart. It's about leveraging the power of digital technologies, embracing an agile mindset, and creating a culture of continuous learning and innovation. It's about staying ahead of the curve in an ever-evolving business landscape, where the fast indeed eats the slow.

Further Information

- Why Agile is Eating The World[61] - Steve Denning. Forbes.
- Why Hardware Must Embrace Agile[62] - Steve Denning. Forbes.
- Agile at Scale[63] - Darrell Rigby, Jeff Sutherland, and Andy Noble. Harvard Business Review.

---

[61]https://www.forbes.com/sites/stevedenning/2018/01/02/why-agile-is-eating-the-world /
[62]https://www.forbes.com/sites/stevedenning/2020/06/21/why-hardware-must-embrace-agile-principles/
[63]https://hbr.org/2018/05/agile-at-scale

How to Start the Transformation

As the Author
I want to show how to start an Agile Transformation
So that readers understand what is important not to forget initially.

Start from Business

Embarking on the Agile transformation journey should begin with a clear understanding of why this shift is necessary for your business. This initial step involves identifying a business justification, which usually resides in the form of business challenges or market opportunities. Analyze your current business operations, competitive landscape, customer demands, and potential risks to identify the pressing need for agility. The business justification is a guiding beacon that shapes the transformation strategy and keeps everyone aligned and motivated throughout the process.

I usually ask the C-levels: "Considering your current market, how much EBITA is worth cutting the time-to-market of 50%? How damaging is it if your competitor cuts their time-to-market by 50%?"

We need to start from that number to drive the consequent decisions. Without a precise number, any objection would have a voice to slow down or make the transformation stall.

Form a Management Team

The next step in initiating an Agile transformation is forming a dedicated management team. Scrum@Scale[64] call this the **EAT - Executive Action Team**. This team is critical to lead the change process, make strategic decisions, solve problems, and drive the organization toward agility. The team should consist of senior leaders who are enthusiastic and committed to the Agile transformation and have influence within the organization. These individuals will champion the cause, demonstrate agile principles in their leadership, and set an example for the rest of the organization. Scrum@Scale suggests that the **Executive Action Team** should, at least, contain the following:

- An executive who can change company policy without asking permission [ex. COO, CIO, CTO]
- Someone who manages the budget and can write a check [ex. VP of Finance]
- Someone who is a Scrum Star [aka. Agile Champion]
- Leaders who can motivate change
- Someone from People Ops [ex. HR]
- Someone from Legal/Compliance [another specialty, ex: Security, regulatory expert, etc.]

Like any other team, the size shouldn't exceed nine; the recommended number is five members.

Train the Management

Before the management team can effectively lead the transformation, they must learn Organizational Design and fully understand Agile principles, values, practices, and benefits. Management

---

[64]https://www.scrumatscale.com/scrum-at-scale-guide-online/

training is vital to equip them with the necessary knowledge and skills. This training is generally in the form of short courses and workshops. Hiring a Senior Agile Coach to work with the Management Team at the beginning and educate them on the less intuitive concepts is highly advisable. The goal is to ensure that management can not only talk about Agile but also live it and guide their teams through it.

Value Sources and Value Stream

A fundamental concept for every organization is delivering value. As such, identifying the sources of value in your organization is crucial. This might include your unique products or services, customer relationships, operational efficiency, or innovative capabilities. Understanding these value sources helps shape your Agile transformation to increase the value delivered to the market.

The following step is to decide where to start the agile adoption. The management team needs to identify the mature value sources, defined often as *Cash Cow*, and the promising future sources, also known as *Rising Stars*.

Where to start?

- Start from Business with a robust discussion about **Today's and Tomorrow's Value sources**.
- Identify the **Cash Cow**, the one who keeps us alive today, and the **Rising Stars**, those who will feed us tomorrow.
- Start with something in the middle: not the Cash Cow but not even something irrelevant, probably a rising star.

©2023 Paolo Sammicheli

SCRUM
@SCALE

Identify a Value Stream

Choose a value stream from your value source mapping to start your Agile transformation. It's advisable to start with a less complex value stream that significantly impacts your business. This way, you can start seeing benefits quickly, learn and adapt before scaling Agile to more complex areas of your organization. On the other hand, you cannot start with something irrelevant; otherwise, solving the impediments wouldn't be a priority. A good idea is to start with something that would become important in the future, probably a *Rising Stars*.

Next, we need to map the Value Stream[65] for the selected source. This means identifying the sequence of steps that create and deliver value to the customer. Value stream mapping helps visualize how value flows through your organization, where bottlenecks or waste occur, and where there are opportunities for improvement. This is described in the next chapter and will serve as a critical tool to start the Pilot Team of your Agile transformation.

Communicate the Initiative

Once you have a plan for a Pilot Team in place, communicate the Agile transformation initiative to all employees. Effective communication ensures everyone understands the transformation's why, what, and how. This step involves explaining the business justification, what Agile is, how it will be implemented, and what benefits it will bring. Transparency and regular updates to the entire workforce will help foster support, engagement, and ownership among everyone.

---

[65]https://en.wikipedia.org/wiki/Value-stream_mapping

Training and Workshops

Conduct training sessions and workshops for employees at all levels to build Agile understanding across the organization. These sessions should cover the theory of Agile and its practical application. Use real-world examples, case studies, and hands-on exercises to help employees understand and apply Agile principles. Remember, transforming into an Agile organization is not just about changing processes but also about changing mindsets.

In conclusion, starting the Agile transformation involves a series of necessary steps, from identifying a business justification to conducting training and workshops. It requires the commitment of the whole organization, but with clear communication, inspiring leadership, and continuous learning, the transformation can lead to significant benefits for your business.

The Pilot Team

As the Author
I want to show how to start a pilot team
So that readers understand how to start.

This chapter illustrates how to start the first pilot team in a company willing to transform itself into an Agile Organization. Pictures from the Sisma and Pietro Fiorentini case study will illustrate the several steps.

Value Stream Mapping and Skill Mapping

The first step of the pilot team is mapping the production stream of the selected value source. A common way of doing that is using Value Stream Mapping.

Value Stream Mapping is a lean-management method that visualizes the current steps and information flows required to deliver a product or service to the customer. This visualization is essential to understanding how your process works and identifying waste or inefficiency areas. To conduct Value Stream Mapping, you walk through every process step, from initial customer request to delivery, noting the time, resources, and information needed at each stage.

VALUE STREAM MAP

- During a workshop involving about 25 people, we mapped all the tasks of the selected Value Stream: **Laser Machining**.

- The value stream map captured all the concept-to-cash activities: from pre-sale until installation and post-sale customer services.

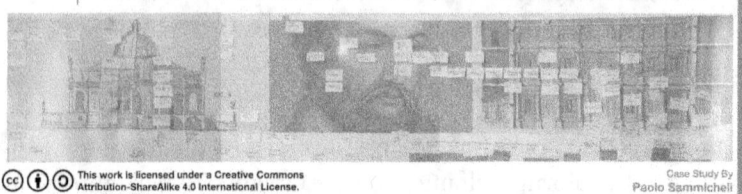

This work is licensed under a Creative Commons
Attribution-ShareAlike 4.0 International License.

Case Study By
Paolo Sammicheli

Example of the VSM - Sisma Case Study

In a Lean approach, we would use this visualization to identify opportunities for reducing waste and improving flow and create a 'future state' map.

In Scrum, we use it, on the other hand, to map the competencies and skills of each step.

SKILL MAPPING

- In the same workshop, for each macro-step of the value stream map, we mapped the needed skills.

- The mapped skills included competencies (hard skills), domain (customer engineering process), and soft skills.

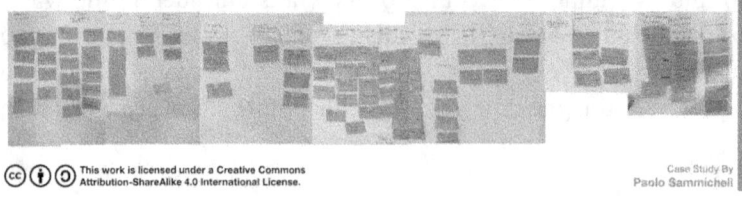

This work is licensed under a Creative Commons
Attribution-ShareAlike 4.0 International License.

Case Study By
Paolo Sammicheli

Example of the Skill Mapping - Sisma Case Study

The Sisma Case Study Value Stream Map was created in a half-day workshop involving about 25 people from different departments. It made it possible to identify the skills necessary to produce value that we aggregated into 15 professional profiles.

Here's the first important nuance: when you do this the first time, people will naturally think about the existing **Roles** (like Mechanical Designer or Tester). A role is a set of responsibilities; it tells you what you must do.

We talk instead about **Professional Profiles** (and following the previous example would be Mechanical Design and Testing) because that is a set of competencies; it tells you what you can do.

We consider people having many roles a problem because it shows poor focus. Instead, a person with many professional profiles is a positive connotation because it signifies seniority and flexibility.

I found this concept hard to grasp initially and often needed to repeat it multiple times during the workshop.

The next step is to create the self-assessment questionnaire with the professional profiles gathered with this exercise. This self-assessment is typically sent to a large audience so that we can start gathering information about the distribution of the skills across the company. In the case of Sisma, we sent it to the entire department, including white and blue collars. We can produce a Skill Matrix card for each employee with the gathered data.

SKILL MATRIX

- The identified skills have been categorized into 15 profiles.
- We asked to the all R&D Department workforce to self evaluate themselves in the 15 profiles, to build their skill matrix.
- Levels vary from Beginner (can operate but with mentoring) to Senior (can operate autonomously) and Master (can teach).

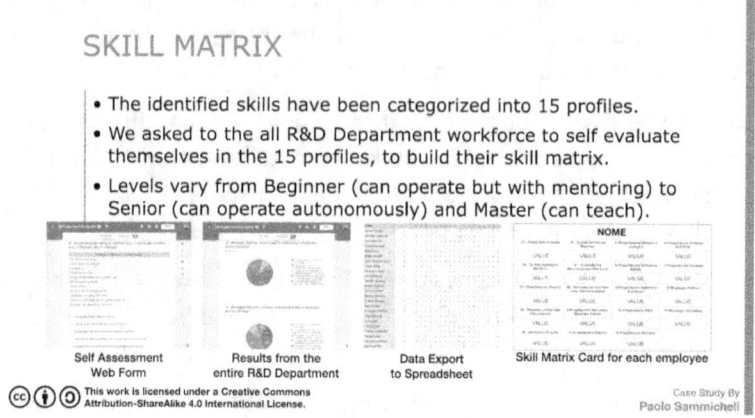

| Self Assessment Web Form | Results from the entire R&D Department | Data Export to Spreadsheet | Skill Matrix Card for each employee |

This work is licensed under a Creative Commons Attribution-ShareAlike 4.0 International License.

Case Study By Paolo Sammicheli

Example of the Skill Matrix - Sisma Case Study

Another problem I often find is that HR and Management want many levels of expertise. I instead insist on having only three:

- **Beginner**. I can work on the professional profile only with mentoring
- **Senior**. I can work on the professional profile autonomously
- **Master**. I can teach and mentor beginners on this professional profile.

That's the only information you need to form Scrum Teams. Adding more levels is not helpful and can distract from other important topics: *vulnerabilities*.

Almost every time I do this exercise in a company, I find a specific competency known only by a particular person or a few. And without that, you cannot deliver value. This is something that needs to be mitigated because not only is most of the time a bottleneck that limits the flow, but it is also a severe threat to the resiliency of the company. One approach to mitigate this problem is to build a team around the bottleneck person and use the Mitosis Pattern, described later with Scaling, to scale up that particular capability.

Printing the employees' cards, you can do a speculative organizational design to brainstorm the possible team composition, see how many teams you can have, and understand weaknesses and areas of improvement.

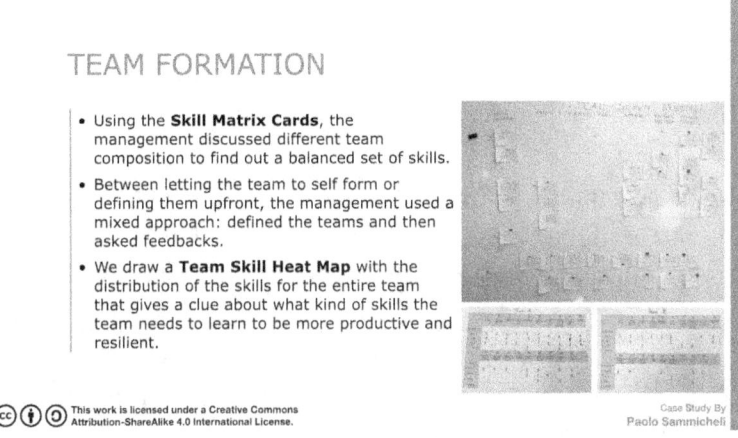

TEAM FORMATION

- Using the **Skill Matrix Cards**, the management discussed different team composition to find out a balanced set of skills.
- Between letting the team to self form or defining them upfront, the management used a mixed approach: defined the teams and then asked feedbacks.
- We draw a **Team Skill Heat Map** with the distribution of the skills for the entire team that gives a clue about what kind of skills the team needs to learn to be more productive and resilient.

This work is licensed under a Creative Commons Attribution-ShareAlike 4.0 International License.

Case Study By
Paolo Sammicheli

Example of the Team Formation - Sisma Case Study

I recommend iterating the speculative organizational design multiple times, involving all the impacted people and collecting feedback from everybody. Forming a team in a top-down approach without a general consensus about the team composition would already signify a lack of understanding of the first Agile Manifesto value, "individual and interaction over processes and tools."

Pilot Team Liftoff

At this point, you might discover that you need more than ten people to deliver value. Since a team of more than ten people is known to be less effective than a smaller one, you will need multiple teams working on the same increment.

The concept of multiple teams working in a coordinated way on the same product is called Scaling in Scrum and is discussed in the following chapters. To make you understand the process of starting the first team, I will consider in this chapter that you can deliver value with less than ten people, leaving the more complex Scrum structure for later. If you lead this kind of transformation for the first time and have multiple value sources to choose from, starting with a Value Stream that can be delivered with less than ten people would be wise.

At this point, you can launch the Pilot Team and perform the Team's Lift Off.

The book "Liftoff - Start and Sustain Successful Agile Teams" by Diana Larsen and Ainsley Nies describes the Liftoff concept for project chartering, which I think is essential in Hardware teams.

For Agile Chartering, we mean a high-level summary of the critical success factors of the project or product, typically elaborated in the form of information radiators, like posters for co-located teams, or virtual boards like miro.com[66] or mural.co[67], for remote teams. According to the Agile Chartering model of the Liftoff book, there are three phases to complete: *Purpose, Alignment, Context.*

Purpose

Purpose is the reason why the initiative is carried out; the activity with this name offers support and inspiration in trying to understand what drives us to create a given product.

The definition of Value

To facilitate the brainstorming of the vision and the value of a project, I developed The Basic Canvas, a variation of Roman Pichler's Product Vision Board[68] that I released under a Creative

---

[66]http://miro.com

[67]http://mural.co

[68]https://www.romanpichler.com/tools/product-vision-board/

Commons license and freely downloadable from my personal website[69].

The Basic Canvas	Project:			Date:
Who is it for?	Needs and Desire	Solution		Expectation
Who is not for?	Obstacles	Alternatives		Risks

This work is licensed under a Creative Commons Attribution-ShareAlike 4.0 International License. To see a copy of the license visit, https://creativecommons.org/licenses/by-sa/4.0/

The Basic Canvas, by Paolo Sammicheli - http://paolo.sammiche.li
Inspired by the work of Alex Osterwalder, Ash Maurya, Roman Pichler, and others.

Basic Canvas

It discusses who our customers are and which aren't their needs, desires, and obstacles to trying to reach them. I believe this scenario is the basic definition of value, represented in the left half of the Canvas. When someone has an impediment to satisfying his desire, they are willing to exchange value with somebody who can help him in his goal. Therefore, the right half of the Canvas allows us to discuss what we can offer to help those listed on the left side achieve their goals and the alternatives to our idea today. The last column captures the Business expectations from the Sponsors of the initiative and the risks in satisfying these ambitions.

---

[69]https://paolo.sammiche.li/download

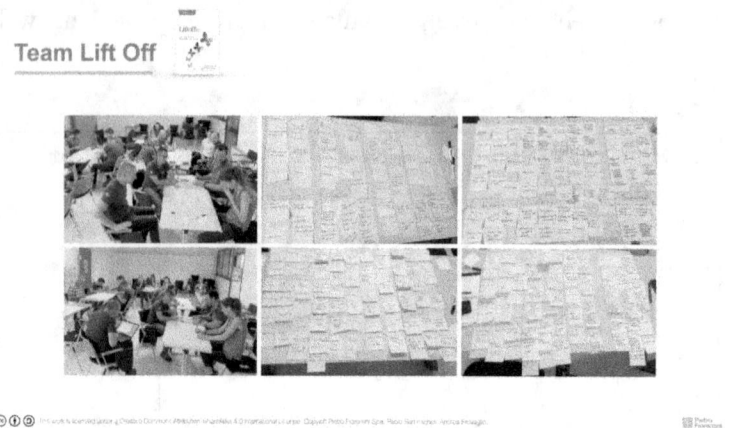

Example of parallel brainstorming - Pietro Fiorentini Case Study

To develop the Basic Canvas, I usually divide the participants into different tables, in which different canvases were created in parallel. Then, on a large wall, we combined the ideas that emerged at each table into the final artifact that remains for the project's duration.

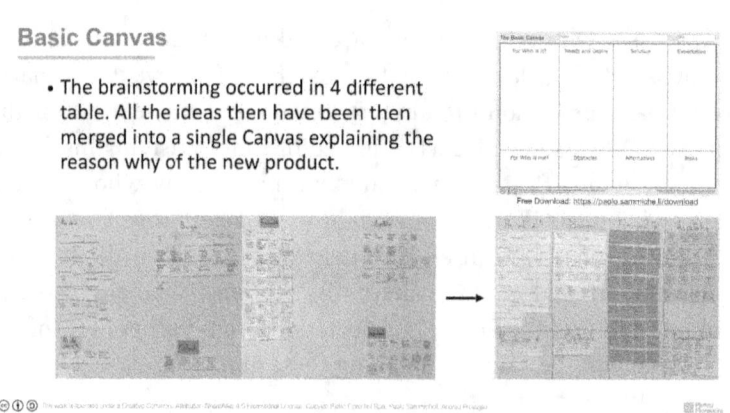

Example of Canvas merging - Pietro Fiorentini Case Study

Alignment

The Alignment step aims to create the alliance that leads to the result described in the Purpose phase. To create an alliance, the initiative's objective must be aligned with the personal objectives of the people who participate. We all win if we win together, or, as stated in the slogan of the Liftoff book, "Came As Individuals, Left As a Team."

The activities envisaged in the Alignment are the identification of the core teams, if necessary, the definition of working agreements, and the definition of values.

In Scrum, there are several Working Agreements:

- The Working Agreement. The set of simple rules that govern the team's life.
- The Definition of Done. The set of criteria that must be respected to consider a job as complete.
- The Definition of Ready. The criterion establishes when the Product Backlog items are sufficiently clear to be eligible for Sprint Planning.

The last described activity is that of identifying team values. Some teams adopt Scrum values: Respect, Courage, Commitment, Openness, and Focus; others prefer to choose their own. It depends a lot on the context: my advice as a coach is to leave the team with complete autonomy.

Context

No man is an island... let alone a team in a company. It is necessary to identify how the nascent initiative is placed in the company context and which interactions it must have with the Single Matter Experts, Stakeholders, and other teams. To do this, creating a chart that illustrates the relationships is beneficial. In this chart, I normally divide into Neighbors - the experts and teams that could help us, and Stakeholders - the people we invite to Sprint Review to get feedback.

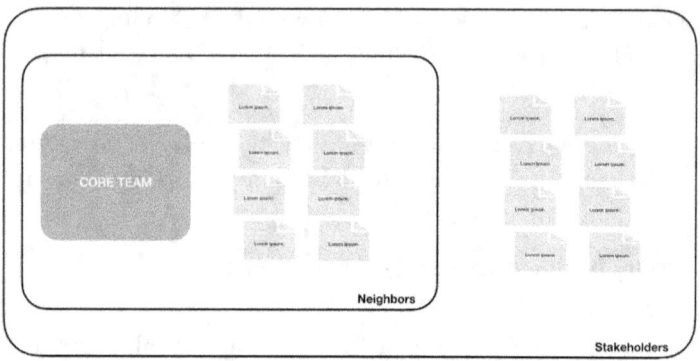

Stakeholders and Neighbors mapping

Other activities of this last step include identifying and discussing available resources (time, external media, budget, workspaces, suppliers and equipment, tools, training, etc.). Another fundamental aspect is the discussion of the product's starting architecture, modules, and interfaces, which are the basis of Agile Architecture. To finish, it is necessary to proceed to a risk analysis activity, for example, listing a set of FUD (Fears, Uncertainties, and Doubts) and then categorizing the items one by one in a ROAM schema: Resolved, Owned, Accepted, Mitigated.

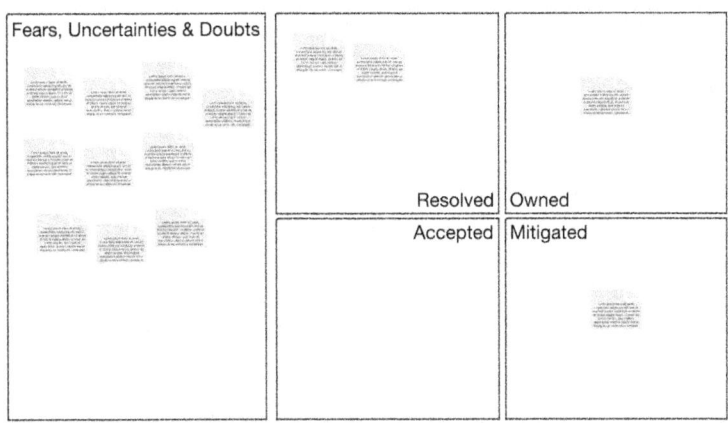

Agile Risk Management example

Last but not least is the team space. If it's a Hardware Team, it will need space to integrate the product and host the Sprint Review. In many companies, they needed to reorganize the rooms significantly.

Example of space organization - Sisma Case Study

Product Backlog Creation

A list of deliverables

The simplest way to create a Product Backlog with Hardware is just to list the deliverables of the project or product. Often people already have this list, so this could be one approach. Be careful not to list the activities or tasks but just the deliverables. Activities reflect the process, and typically, if you're starting the first team, that would be a waterfall development in the form of a stage and gate. Listing the deliverables allows the team to challenge the process and get the same result in better ways.

A wall of tests

Another interesting approach is what Joe Justice did with the Wikispeed[70] Backlog. In 2011, Wikispeed goal was to participate in the Automotive XPrice building a 100mpg car, meaning 100 Miles per Gallon equivalent. So they started with two high-level goals: Build a fuel-efficient car and meet the read safety requirements. From that high-level goals, he created a set of tests and experiments.

---

[70]The Wikispeed Case Study is available in the appendix of the book.

Wikispeed Product Backlog

Wikispeed initial Backlog. Courtesy Joe Justice

Joe defines this approach as a "wall of tests." A set of conditions to become true to achieve the goal.

If your product is user interactive and you want to use a user-centric development approach, you can alternatively use the same techniques as software teams and create user stories. Following the techniques I consider more effective.

Seven Dimensions

The "7 Dimension" technique is described in the Discovery to Deliver[71] book by Ellen Gottesdiener and Mary Gorman. I learned this technique from Scrum Inc's Product Owner class, so even Jeff Sutherland recommends it. The Seven Dimensions facilitate the conversation with the stakeholders in a workshop, in this case, the final part of the LiftOff. Still, it could also be used further to slice a User Story during a Product Backlog Refinement.

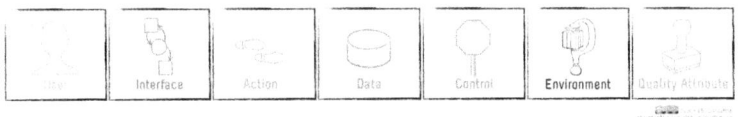

---

[71]https://www.discovertodeliver.com

Some dimensions (USER, ACTION, DATA, and CONTROL) are about Functional Requirements: they define specific behaviors, actions, or interactions with the system. The remaining ones (INTERFACE, ENVIRONMENT, and QUALITY) are Nonfunctional Requirements, meaning that they define the criteria and characteristics of the system. The visual tool aims to guide through questions that help elicit the requirements and needs from a user's point of view. Let's see the dimensions with the related questions I use to facilitate the conversation during the workshop.

User

What are the users that will interact with the Product? What is their background? What is the goal they want to achieve? Another technique I sometimes use in combination with this section is the User Persona[72].

Interface

What are the interfaces that will connect the users with the system? This dimension may relate to the environment where the user will access the Product. Is it going to be an office application only? Is it also Mobile? Or maybe it's not even an application: the user wants only to be notified by email with a weekly report.

Action

What Actions will be required from the users to provide the needed capabilities? Is there a specific workflow? How is an action triggered? How does the Product respond? How do actions impact Data?

---

[72]https://en.wikipedia.org/wiki/Persona_(user_experience)

Data

What source of Data will be involved to provide the highlighted capability? How often do we need to update it? Who could help to annotate it? How do you know whether the Data is valid or not?

Control

What are the Controls we need to perform? What are the risks if the Product does not comply with the control needs? Is there any limitation and privacy/security concerns with the Data?

Environment

What are the physical properties and the technological platforms involved? Where will the user be when using our application? On which kind of device?

Quality Attribute

What are the quality attributes? Many of the FURPS[73] quality attributes apply, like Functionality, Usability, Reliability, Performance, Security, and others.

As we noticed, the Product Dimensions focus on one aspect of the Product, so they depend on other Dimensions. The book shows a Canvas to highlight these relationships.

---

[73]https://en.wikipedia.org/wiki/FURPS

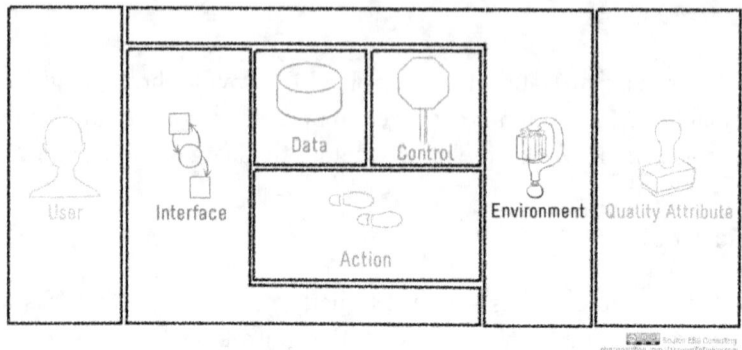

For each dimension, you should brainstorm all the possible alternatives. Then highlighting the high-priority elements in each dimension, you can forge the first set of user stories to build the MVP[74].

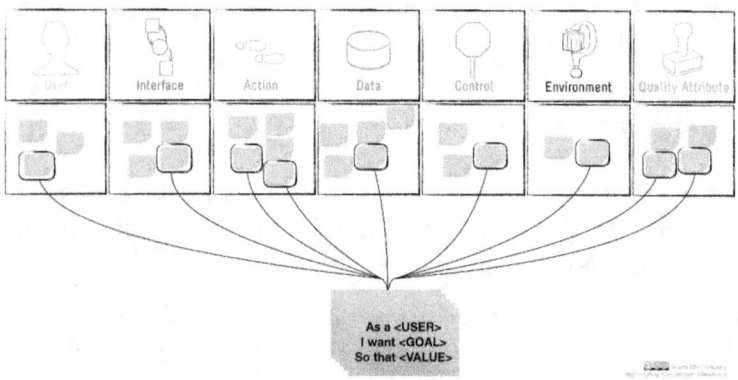

The USER and ACTION dimensions help draft the User Story, which stays on the front of the card, together with the VALUE statement. The remaining dimensions are used to create the Acceptance Criteria, traditionally on the back of the card. Section 3 of the book Discovery to Deliver, freely downloadable from their website[75], contains a detailed description of each dimension.

---

[74]https://en.wikipedia.org/wiki/Minimum_viable_product
[75]https://www.discovertodeliver.com/download.php

User Story Mapping

User Story Mapping[76] is a brainstorming technique invented and popularized by Jeff Patton[77]. It organizes the different features on a bi-dimensional map that supports a rich conversation with stakeholders and allows the grouping of features in releases.

If I have a significant part of the audience that never worked with this practice, I start with the following warm-up [78].

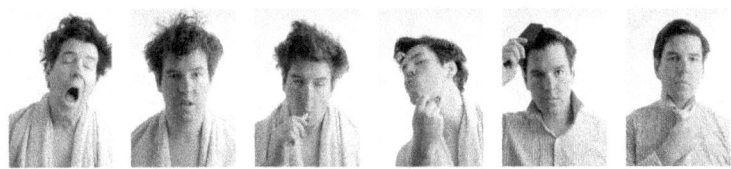

I ask some participants to write sticky notes with their actions from when they woke up to when they got into the office (or online, if remote working), one thing per sticky note. Then we arrange the sticky notes horizontally, in chronological order, on a large wall, and combine actions from the different participants, removing duplicates. The order doesn't need to be strictly chronological; some people do breakfast and then shower, and others do vice versa. This way, we get a list of items in a plausible chronological order. At that point, we create clusters by putting a label over them, like "food," "personal hygiene," clothing, etc., getting something like the following picture:

Then I pick up a participant and ask: "Imagine you wake up one hour late; what action would you take anyway? Move them down

---

[76]https://www.jpattonassociates.com/story-mapping/

[77]https://www.jpattonassociates.com/about-jeff-patton-associates/

[78]Images from Aaron Sanders slides https://www.slideshare.net/aaronsanders/passionate-product-ownership Creative Commons BY-NC-SA

one row." This way, we get the essential items under the commonly performed items. "Now, imagine you wake up with the sound of the fire alarm; what action would you take anyway? Move them down one row more." At that point, we get three lists: actions usually done, activities done even when late, and essential activities. I use these two questions to show participants that prioritization is always possible and how to identify different releases by vertically arranging the activities.

Finally, we can start brainstorming the features of the actual product. The main backbone comprises user tasks that represent the user's journey through the product, so we start from that. Depending on the grain size of the user tasks you identify during the brainstorming, you can group them and add a label, like in the ice break exercise, or split them into activities if they are gross-grained. Some people identify these different grains with Epic, Feature, and Story helpful. I usually don't stress the terminology too much since other books use it differently (for some authors, Epic is bigger than a Feature; for others, it is vice versa). In the end, you will have a bi-dimensional map of user actions representing the features of your product. The following picture shows an example of the Vimar Case Study user story mapping. The product, a smart-home platform, has been mapped considering two users: the person living in the house and the electrician installing the product.

Whole team alignment

Every project start with at least **two day of LiftOff**, with the whole team, the key stakeholders and some managers, where we share the Vision, the requirements, the constraints and we create the first backlog with the **User Story Mapping** technique, covering Software and Hardware layers.

This work is licensed under a Creative Commons Attribution-ShareAlike 4.0 International License.

Case Study By
Paolo Sammicheli

User Story Mapping - Vimar Case Study

With User Story Mapping, you can build your Product Backlog, where the ordering of the story is by priority. Many product owners maintain the user story mapping to keep reflecting on the different features since it's not convenient to reflect on new features directly on your priority ordered list in the Product Backlog. Some Agile Tools allow maintaining the two views synchronized, which is helpful to monitor development; for this regard, Jeff Patton recommends in his material tagging stories to show progress[79], as shown in the following picture as an example.

---

[79]Image from Jeff Patton's "Passionate Product Leadership" handouts https://www.jpattonassociates.com/handouts/ Creative Commons BY-NC-SA

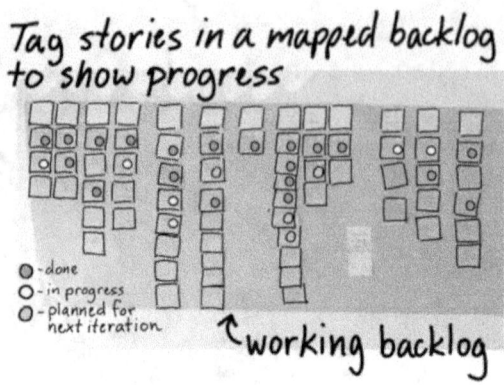

Impact Mapping

Impact Mapping is a Product Backlog elicitation technique by Gojko Adzic, published in 2014 in his book "Impact Mapping Making a big impact with software products and projects[80]." Gojco says that Impact mapping is a variant of the InUse effect mapping method[81], introduced by Mijo Balic and Ingrid Domingues (Ottersten), combined with:

- Impact Maps for training organizations[82] invented by Robert O. Brinkerhoff
- The Feature Injection ideas[83] of Chris Matts
- The Measurability and Iterative Delivery ideas[84] of Tom Gilb[85].

---

[80]https://www.goodreads.com/book/show/16084015-impact-mapping
[81]https://www.inuse.se/read/birth-impact-mapping/
[82]https://www.innovativelg.com/user_area/content_media/raw/Impact_Mapping_WhitePaper_Final.pdf
[83]https://www.infoq.com/articles/feature-injection-success/
[84]http://concepts.gilb.com/dl792
[85]https://en.wikipedia.org/wiki/Tom_Gilb

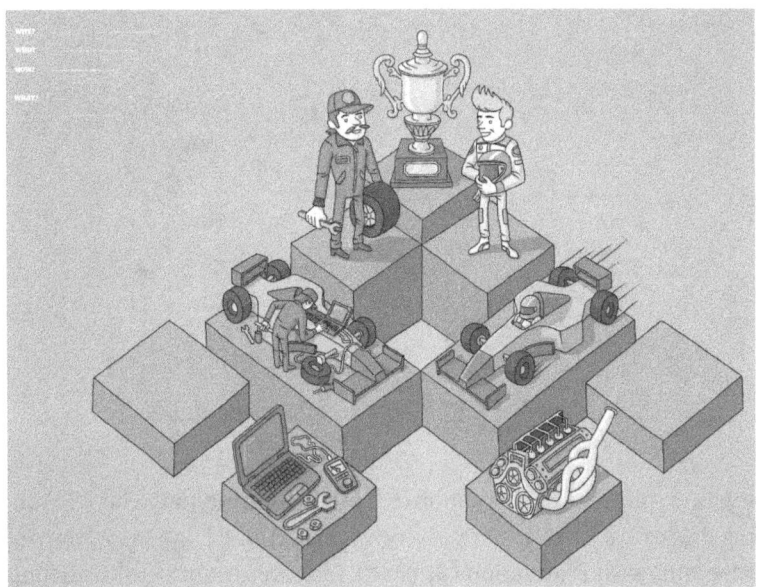

An impact mapping is a visual tool to collaboratively share the scope and underlying assumptions between technical and business people. It is a Mind Map[86] created during a discussion facilitated by answering the following four questions:

1. Why?
2. Who?
3. How?
4. What?

The following image shows an example from the Open Source Workshop Material[87] published by the Author.

---

[86]https://en.wikipedia.org/wiki/Mind_map
[87]https://github.com/impactmapping/open-impact-mapping-workshop

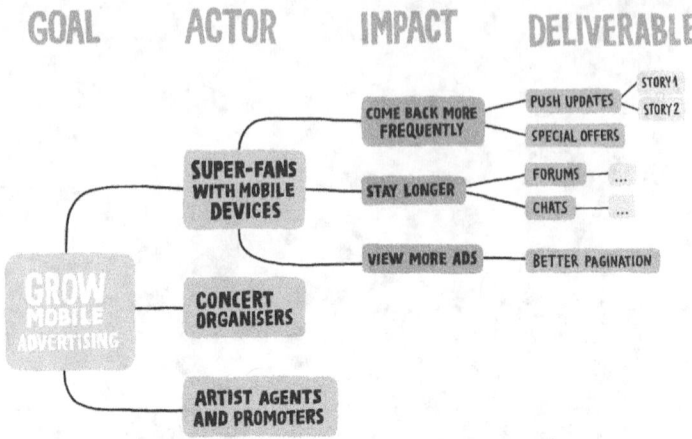

I was inspired to try this approach after listening to Gojco explaining it during the keynote of the Italian Agile Day 2016 "Impact Mapping with Innovation Games[88]." I highly recommend watching this video. It's informative and, at some traits, funny.

Coaching the Pilot Team

At this point, you have a Pilot Team formed. This means that you have:

- A group of developers allocated to the team full-time
- A Product Owner and a Scrum Master
- A clear Purpose, known and agreed upon with management and every team member.
- A set of rules that the team agreed on, like DoD, Dor, etc.
- A Product Backlog, with all the high-level deliverables and around one month's worth of work properly refined in items shorter than one week.

_____
[88]https://gojko.net/2016/12/15/impact-mapping-iad.html

If one or more elements are "ready, but" (ex, we have developers but allocated 50%), you should treat this as a symptom and go back to understand the root cause. Starting the pilot with known dysfunction and not raising them at the beginning with the management team is an original sin that you will pay with for the rest of the transition. Let me rephrase this, trying to be clear:

> If the organization can't even start with a small Scrum Team without significant dysfunctions from day 0, that company probably shouldn't even start the Agile transformation.

You can quote me on this. Often, I get the objection that a person can't be on the team full-time because other duties cannot be left behind. The answer is simple: write that duty on a Post-it and give it to the Product Owner. In an Agile Organization, activities flow to stable teams, and it's not people chasing activities around.

So, it's time to set expectations on timing. Considering a two-week sprint cadence, what I ask management for the first four sprints (first two months) is the suspension of judgment. While studying coaching at the beginning of my career, I've been told that to form a habit, you need 21 days. However, a 2009 study[89] has described the 21-day habit formation formula as a myth. According to Phillippa Lally, a health psychology researcher at University College London, a new habit usually takes a little more than two months — 66 days to be exact — and as much as 254 days until it's fully formed.

In my career, I've seen teams starting very well in the first four Sprints and then getting into trouble, and others starting very slowly in the first sprints and then getting to performance.

So, in the first four Sprints, I recommend insisting on removing impediments, getting to know each other, building trust, supporting

---

[89]"How are habits formed: Modelling habit formation in the real world" - Phillippa Lally, Cornelia H. M. van Jaarsveld, Henry W. W. Potts, Jane Wardle: https://onlinelibrary.wiley.com/doi/abs/10.1002/ejsp.674

the team members in getting the new habits, and inspiring them on what it means to be a high-performing team. Depending on the company culture, I might maintain the Sprint Reviews on invitation only and safe-to-fail, inviting only supporting and friendly stakeholders.

At Sprint Four, I ask the team to reflect on their process, eventually with a self-assessment described later for Sprint 8. From Sprint Five, I usually start having public Sprint Reviews with real stakeholders. At Sprint Eight, we do a special retrospective with Scrum Inc's self-assessment.

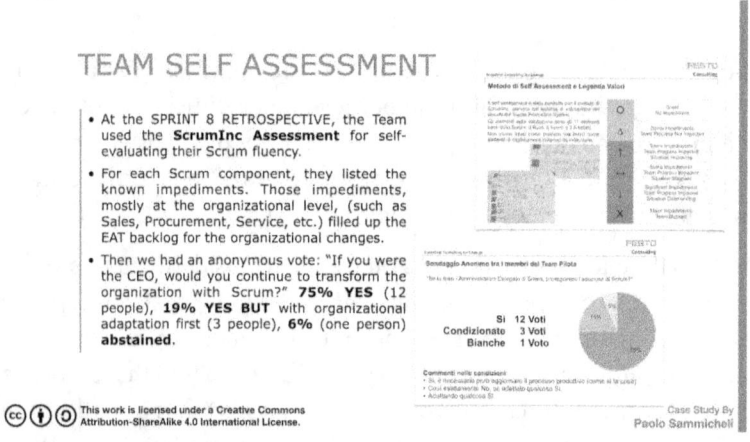

Example the Team Self-Assessment - Sisma Case Study

I ask the team to elicit the impediments and dysfunctions for each Scrum element (3 Roles, 5 Events, 3 Artefacts). Then for each element, considering the number of impediments, I ask them to agree on the rating between the following values:

1. O (green) - Great. No Impediment.
2. Δ (yellow) - Some Impediments. Team Progress Not Impacted.
3. ↑ (red) - Some Impediments. Team Progress Impacted, Situation Improving.

4. ↔ (red) - Some Impediments. Team Progress Impacted, Situation Stagnant.
5. ↓ (red) - Significant Impediments. Team Progress Impacted, Situation Deteriorating.
6. X (violet) - Major Impediments. Team Blocked.

Then I ask the team to divide the impediments between the sphere of control (things they can fix themselves) and the sphere of influence (things they can ask somebody to fix it). The things within the sphere of control become retrospective actions, while the sphere of influence with the color code is published to the management as the pilot result.

As the last activity, I ask the people to anonymously vote on "If you were the CEO of this company, would you continue to transform the organization with Scrum?." With this data, it's time to gather the transformation team (aka Executive Action Team) and decide the next step. The decision typically spans the following options:

- The Pilot Team data is not convincing; let's reiterate the experiment with another team/value stream. Normally without disbanding the first team, so that it remains as a reference.
- The Pilot Team data is convincing, but we want more evidence, so let's start a few more teams and continue collecting data.
- The Pilot Team data is convincing; let's transform the adjacent value streams and build an Agile Business Unit.

Other times it happens that the sponsor of the initiative move elsewhere, or politics plays their cards to maintain the status quo, and nothing happens for a while or forever. I've seen companies starting and stopping the transformation for years without progressing significantly. Traditional organizations have more bureaucracy, useless processes, and privileged positions of power; if the people benefit from that system are a significant number, their influence on maintaining things like they are might be effective.

After all, as we said in the previous chapters, achieving Industrial Agility is a competitive advantage. How could it be a competitive advantage if it was easy and for everybody?

Further readings

- Liftoff: Launching Agile Teams & Projects[90] - Diana Larsen, Ainsley Nies
- Impact Mapping: Making a Big Impact with Software Products and Projects[91] - Gojko Adzic
- User Story Mapping: Discover the Whole Story, Build the Right Product[92] - Jeff Patton, Peter Economy
- Specification by Example[93] - Gojko Adzic
- Discovery to Delivery[94] - Ellen Gottesdiener, Mary Gorman

---

[90]https://www.goodreads.com/book/show/13493815-liftoff
[91]https://www.goodreads.com/book/show/16084015-impact-mapping
[92]https://www.goodreads.com/book/show/22221112-user-story-mapping
[93]https://www.goodreads.com/book/show/10288718-specification-by-example
[94]https://www.discovertodeliver.com/download.php

Agile Architecture

As the Author
I want to discuss what Agile Architecture means
So that the readers understand Conway's Law implications.

Before discussing Scaling in the next chapter, we must explore the relationship between the product architecture and the organization.

Conway's Law

Conway's law states that organizations will create systems that reflect their communication structure. Melvin Conway, a computer scientist, proposed this concept in 1967. His original phrase was as follows:

> Any organization that designs a system will produce a design whose structure is a copy of the organization's communication structure.

A Massachusetts Institute of Technology (MIT) Team and Harvard Business School researchers published evidence supporting Conway's law[95]. They claimed that the "product developed by the loosely-coupled organization is significantly more modular than the product developed by the tightly-coupled organization," using "the mirroring hypothesis" as an equivalent term for Conway's law. The authors emphasize the significance of "organizational design decisions on the technical structure of the objects that these organizations generate afterward."

---

[95]https://en.wikipedia.org/wiki/Conway%27s_law#Supporting_evidence

Elon Musk on Agile Architecture

I found an excellent explanation of Conway's Law and an incredibly inspiring introduction to the Agile Architecture principles in the "A conversation with Elon Musk about Starship[96]" interview from the Everyday Astronaut[97] youtube channel.

Following is an adapted transcript of the significant parts of Elon Musk's perspective, divided by topics:

Simple Design

> I think I've learned a lot of lessons about how to make things go fast. And then I've propagated those lessons to the SpaceX team, and there's just like an incredibly talented, hard-working team at SpaceX. We have taken the general approach of **"if a design is taking too long, the design is wrong,"** and therefore, the design must be modified to accelerate progress. And one of the most fundamental errors made in advanced developments is

[96]https://www.youtube.com/watch?v=cIQ36Kt7UVg
[97]https://www.youtube.com/channel/UC6uKrU_WqJ1R2HMTY3LIx5Q

to stick to a design, even when it is very complicated, and not strive to delete parts and processes.

Who's the Chief Engineer?

I was actually at dinner with a friend, and he was like, "Well, who's the chief engineer at SpaceX?"
I said, "It's me." - "No, no," he's like, "It's not you, who is it?"
And I replied, "Okay, it's either someone with a very low ego or, I don't know."
You know, what I actually used to tell the team is: **"Everyone is a Chief Engineer."**
This is extremely important that everyone must understand how, broadly speaking, all the systems in the vehicle work.

Conway's Law

And so that you don't have self-system optimization, because this is naturally what happens, you can see **"the product errors reflect the organizational errors."** So, like essentially, you'll see that there's an interface at this particular, like, whatever departments you've got, that will be where your interfaces are. Instead of getting rid of something or questioning the constraints, one department will design to the constraints that the other department has given them without calling into question those constraints and saying, "Those constraints are wrong." You should actually take the approach that the constraints you are given are guaranteed to be some degree wrong because the counterpoint would be that they are perfect, which is never.

Perfection doesn't exist

As you were saying like, what's the probability that this is a platonic ideal of a perfect part? Zero, okay, so question your constraints. It does not matter if the person handing you those constraints won a Nobel Prize. Even our own standards are wrong some of the time. So, question your constraints; this is extremely important. Another thing is, "What are the mistakes that smart engineers make?" **One of the biggest traps for smart engineers is optimizing something that shouldn't exist.**

Questions More than Answers

When you go through college, and you're like studying physics or engineering, I studied physics, you have to answer the professor's question; you don't get to say, "This is the wrong question." But, in reality, we have far more degrees. When you're in reality, you have all the degrees of freedom of reality, and so the first thing you should say is, "This question is wrong." It took ages to frame the question. I think it's just like "The Hitchhiker's Guide to the Galaxy" by Douglas Adams, the best philosophy book ever. His book is so deep that people don't even understand. But like, in The Hitchhiker's Guide to the Galaxy, the Earth is a giant computer, and it comes up with the answer "42" to the question "What's the answer to life, the universe, and everything?" The answer's 42, and they say, "What the hell, that doesn't make any sense." So **the really hard part is the question, and the answer is the easy part,** you need a much more powerful computer to tell you what the question is, and this is true at the point in which you can properly frame the question, the answer is comparatively easy.

Agile Architecture principles

Given Conway's Law, evaluating an organizational architecture without having the product architecture on the side and vice-versa is conceptually wrong. The two will influence each other, and the strongest will drive the other. Since the purpose of any company is to deliver frictionless value to customers, the organization should be the simplest human structure to deliver value through a product. Let's look at some product architecture principles in Agile terms.

What is an Agile Architecture

If we go back to Alistair Cockburn's definition of Agile, "the ability to move and change direction, quickly and with ease," an Agile Architecture is the one that makes it easy to change and improve the product or, like Craig Larman[98] often repeat, "to turn on a dime for a dime." This means that *Design for Change* is more important than design for perfection at the first strike.

So, if the architecture is fully emergent, in some way evolutionary, does this mean you shouldn't make any up-front design decisions? The truth is that Architecture, in Agile terms, is *"the set of all the decisions that you cannot not take."* You will always have some decisions to make upfront.

Modularity

The typical Agile approach encapsulates these design decisions that you *cannot not take* into modules. What is a module? Joe Justice, the founder of the Wikispeed[99] project, helped me understand the difference between a Module and a Component. The product in the Wikispeed project is a fuel-efficient car, and it's the first example I show in my first book, "Scrum for Hardware."

---

[98]https://en.wikipedia.org/wiki/Craig_Larman
[99]The case study of Wikispeed is available in the appendix.

Modules vs Components

Let's define a product module as a means to deliver value the customer perceives. A component, conversely, would be a convenient way to separate elements, given their technical nature. An easy example of this concept is Wikispeed architecture.

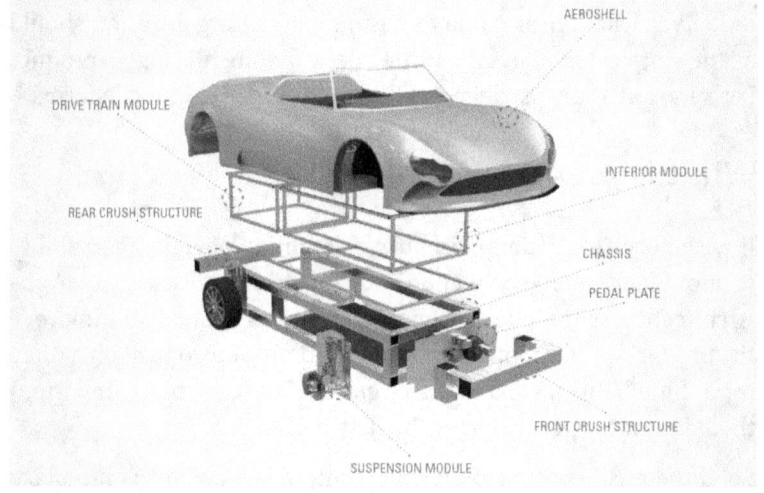

The aeroshell, for example, is a module because it serves all the requirements of aesthetics and aerodynamics. Likewise, the suspension serves all the stability, comfort, and safety needs. On the other hand, the brakes are a component because they do not fulfill a user requirement.

The principle is to have Product Backlog Items impacting one or as few modules as possible. This enables teams to work on different modules during the same Sprint without interfering with each other.

Identifying all the product modules would be challenging initially because this means knowing all the product requirements and crafting a clear Product Backlog in advance.

Joe Justice suggests starting with the most uncomplicated possible design, giving it to a Scrum Team, and letting them iterate and evolve the architecture. This suggestion perfectly matches Elon Musk's interview's "Simple Design" Principe.

Contract First Design

So, let's pretend you have a speculative design of the modules of your product. Then, you start building one module after the other, right? Well, not exactly.

The first step would be to build the scaffold of every module, starting from the interfaces. This approach is called "Contract First Design."

Contract First Design means defining the interface between modules and building the simplest form of the module, starting from the interface. It's vital to coach the Developers to allow space for growth in the interface, anticipate possible evolutions, and create a "decoupling strategy" to develop any module independently (See Dependencies First[100] Pattern).

When somebody working on a Module recognizes the need to change the interface, the process is to "Stop the Line[101]," collect all the people involved around the interface, agree on a new interface, implement the change, and then get back to work.

My perspective is that the Contract First Design is not something that you **build on the product**, but is more a *process* to define and update the agreements between modules as soon as this is needed.

While I was reflecting on this topic to write this chapter, somebody on my LinkedIn network posted: "Coupling is highly problematic. This applies to teams even more than code."

James Coplien[102] commented in a way that caught my attention: "This is a common naive generalization and simplification. Essential

---

[100]http://scrumbook.org/value-stream/sprint-backlog/dependencies-first.html
[101]https://en.wikipedia.org/wiki/Andon_(manufacturing)
[102]https://en.wikipedia.org/wiki/Jim_Coplien

coupling is what builds relationships. Accidental coupling only gets in the way. The goal is not to reduce coupling. The goal is to reduce accidental coupling while leveraging essential coupling to your advantage."

Focussing on the essential coupling while reducing the unneeded coupling is a fascinating principle.

With a **Loosely Coupled Product Architecture**, companies can reduce time-to-market and upgrade their product to maintain them future-proof. Lastly, this enables a loosely coupled relationship with the organizational structure if you leverage the other significant constraint of scaling the product organization: Skillsets.

Skills and Teams

With a modularized product, you can theoretically develop them in parallel, dramatically reducing time-to-market. A simplistic approach would be to assign one team for each module and hope not to get oversized Product Backlog Items where heavy development affects multiple modules.

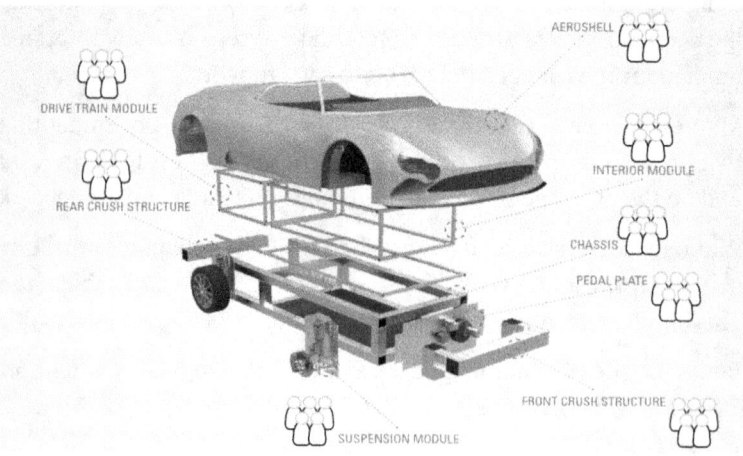

But with an organization like this, how could they "question the constraints" the other teams gave?

The approach would be the same as with an individual to develop compencies but for the entire team. Every team should self-assess the ability to work in each module with the same three levels:

- Junior - we can work on the module, but with somebody mentoring us
- Senior - we can work on the module
- Master - somebody of us can mentor another team on this module

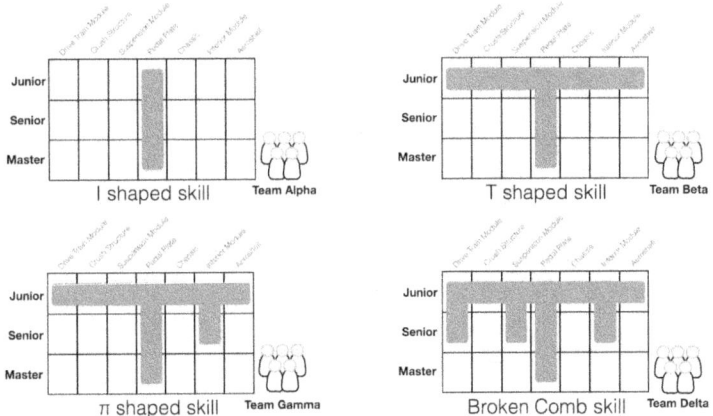

In Large Scale Scrum[103], a team like the Alpha is called a "Component Team," while Teams like Beta, Gamma, and Delta are called Features Teams.

It will be critical to have only teams like the Gamma and the Delta to scale up the organization and maintain innovation and a really evolutionary approach to the product architecture. However, compositions like Team Alpha would be problematic since they might become a bottleneck or remain without enough high-priority

---

[103]https://less.works/less/structure/feature-teams

work. At the same time, something like the Team Beta would be acceptable when transitioning to the "π Shaped Skill."

Skillset is the ultimate constraint when you design organizations. Learning a new skill takes time, and people have preferences and different attitudes, so it's a long, slow, and difficult process. Therefore, it's critical to highlight the bottlenecks in terms of skillsets and to implement all the possible measures to enable the organization to keep learning continuously.

Multiple Teams and Vendors

As the Author
I want to discuss scaling with Scrum
So that readers understand how to scale up with multiple teams and vendors without losing agility.

When you have a value stream that needs more than ten developers, you need what, in Scrum, we call "Scaling."

In this book, I will explain Scrum@Scale as a scaling framework for various reasons:

- It is the framework I know better since I learned it from its author, and today I teach it.
- It is a scaling framework that is not natively related to software and applies to hardware as it is.
- It is based on the Scrum Patterns that I consider the best resource in the Scrum literature.

Other frameworks I recommend are Nexus[104], by Ken Schwaber, and LeSS[105], by Craig Larman. I don't recommend any other scaling framework. If you're working with one of those frameworks other than the three I mentioned and are happy with that, good for you! But if you see dysfunctions that lead to the old status quo, don't complain or tell me I didn't warn you.

---

[104]https://www.scrum.org/resources/scaling-scrum
[105]https://less.works

The first consideration is to scale only when you absolutely need it; a single Scrum Team working on the entire product would be the best option. This quote from the paragraph Scaling Sequence[106] from the Scrum Pattern Books[107] recaps the essence of this concept.

> Scaling is not about transforming an existing micromanaged organization into an Agile one. When someone asks, "We have over 500 developers: how do we scale to Scrum?" is an example of someone asking the wrong question.
>
> How do they know they need 500 developers? And "scaling" is not a proper response to a product that is late in delivery. Brook's Law[108] —that adding people to a late project makes it later— still applies at the team level.
>
> Scaling is about the piecemeal growth of the Development Teams in response to the growth of the product itself. Scrum has always scaled in that sense.
>
> Jeff Sutherland started the first multi-team Scrum at IDX in 1994. Exactly how Scrum scales is mainly situational, but the following patterns are common.

Team of Teams

What does *Team of Teams* means? If a Team is a "group of individuals working together and helping each other reach the common goal," a *Team of Teams* is a "group of Teams working together and helping each other reach the common goal."

---

[106]http://scrumbook.org/product-organization-pattern-language/a-scaling-sequence.html
[107]http://scrumbook.org
[108]https://en.wikipedia.org/wiki/Brooks%27s_law

Scrum of Scrums

In the Scrum@Scale framework[109], this concept is called Scrum of Scrums[110], and it is described in the pattern with the same name.

> When multiple teams work independently of each other, they tend to focus myopically on their own concerns and lose sight of any common goals.
>
> Therefore
>
> Give the right and the responsibility to collaborate on delivering common goals identified by the Product Owner to the Development Teams themselves. Permit the teams to figure out the best way to coordinate their efforts.

The critical aspect is that this pattern gives "the right and the responsibility to collaborate on delivering common goals ... to the Development Teams themselves."

This is the essence, in my opinion: it's not a paternalistic approach where managers organize and coordinate multiple teams, but Developers with the maturity and the duty to find the best way to coordinate the development with the Managers.

The need for coordination between multiple teams leads to the implementation of patterns like:

- Sprinting at the same cadence (Organizational Sprint Pulse[111]).
- Maintaining a common Definition of Done[112].

---

[109]https://www.scrumatscale.com

[110]https://sites.google.com/a/scrumplop.org/published-patterns/product-organization-pattern-language/scrum-of-scrums

[111]http://scrumbook.org/product-organization-pattern-language/organizational-sprint-pulse.html

[112]http://scrumbook.org/value-stream/definition-of-done.html

- Common Scaled Events, like Sprint Planning[113], Sprint Review[114], Product Backlog Refinement[115], and Sprint Retrospective[116].
- Scaled Daily Scrum[117], with representatives from each team, just after the teams' Daily Scrum to resolve emergent dependencies and issues.

Daily Meetings and Scaled Daily

- From 8.30 to 9.00 all the teams have their individual Daily Meeting.
- At 9.00 a representatives from all the teams, also the remotes and suppliers, join the Scrum of Scrum.
- Scrum of Scrums have a senior manager serving as the **Scrum of Scrums Master**, in charge of systemic impediments.

This work is licensed under a Creative Commons Attribution-ShareAlike 4.0 International License.

Case Study By Paolo Sammicheli

Scaled Daily Scrum - Vimar Case Study

To foster collaboration and maintain the ability to "Work together and help each other," I found it beneficial to create at Sprint Planning a buffer for interruptions[118] in every Sprint Backlog and perform the Emergency Procedure[119] pattern as soon as one team encounter an issue.

With the increase in the number of teams and the maturity of the

---

[113]http://scrumbook.org/value-stream/sprint-planning.html

[114]http://scrumbook.org/value-stream/sprint-review.html

[115]http://scrumbook.org/value-stream/product-backlog/refined-product-backlog.html

[116]http://scrumbook.org/value-stream/sprint/sprint-retrospective.html

[117]http://scrumbook.org/value-stream/sprint/daily-scrum.html

[118]http://scrumbook.org/product-organization-pattern-language/illegitimus-non-interruptus.html

[119]http://scrumbook.org/product-organization-pattern-language/emergency-procedure.html

product, it will be helpful to organize a Release Plan[120] event so that both developers and stakeholders have the visibility and the understanding of the midterm goals, maintaining the releases to production small and frequent (Responsive Deployment[121] pattern).

A simple Scrum of Scrums example is in the Sisma Case Study, where we formed a Team of Teams of two. Most members had an electronic background in that case study, so I used the microprocessor metaphor and called it the "Dual Core" Team.

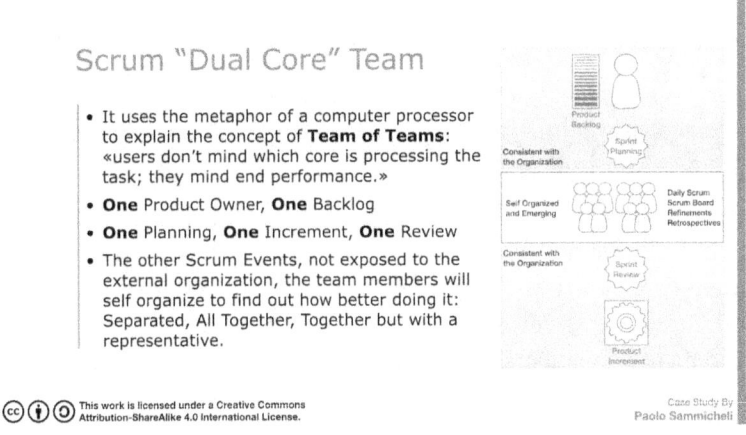

Scaled Pilot Team - Sisma Case Study

Mitosis

Starting a new product from scratch will be difficult, with multiple teams from the beginning. At the genesis of a product, multiple design decisions on the architecture must be made, and too many people would not serve the purpose. An approach I found helpful is to form a first team composed of the most senior people in the main areas of the value stream map to design and implement the first prototype. Then, using the mitosis pattern, grow into a Team of Teams.

---

[120]http://scrumbook.org/value-stream/release-plan.html
[121]http://scrumbook.org/value-stream/responsive-deployment.html

> One should grow a Scrum Team in an incremental, piecemeal fashion, but eventually, the team just becomes too large to remain efficient
>
> Therefore
>
> Differentiate a single large Development Team into two small teams after it gradually grows to the point of inefficiency—about seven people in the old team.

The idea of the Mitosis pattern is to use the biological approach of splitting a development team in two while adding new people to the new teams. In this way, there will always be somebody from the original team within the new team, and with new people, they will become high-performing and capable of working on the entire product over time.

According to Jeff Sutherland, the ideal number of a Scrum team is five. This number comes from a study [122] showing the perfect number to be an average of 4.6 members[123], so as soon as you exceed the number six, you should start splitting the team[124], eventually adding new members to maintain the team cross-functionality.

Initial
Team

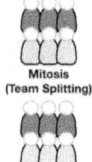

Mitosis
(Team Splitting)

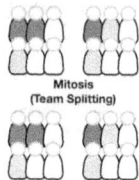

Mitosis
(Team Splitting)

In this example, we move from a team of six developers to an organization of 24 people with two mitoses. The benefit of this approach is that in each team, after the second mitosis, at least one person is from the original team of six. This maintains the memory of decisions made in the initial design in every team.

---

[122]Hackman & Vidmar (1970). Effects of Size and Task Type on Group Performance and Member Reactions. Sociometry. https://doi.org/10.2307/2786271

[123]https://money.cnn.com/magazines/fortune/fortune_archive/2006/06/12/8379238/

[124]https://www.scruminc.com/scrum-keep-team-size-under-7/

How long does it take to maintain a team intact before splitting? Considering what we discussed in the Coaching the Pilot Team chapter, I would not recommend any team change, like adding new people or splitting the teams more frequently than every four or six months.

If your time expectation is shorter and the product is so complex that it cannot be done with less than ten people, remember, "Nine women can't make a baby in one month." Adding more people wouldn't help you.

Product Owner Team

When you have multiple teams, you might have a Product Owner for each team. Certainly, you want them to work together like they were one team. For this reason, you will need the Product Owner Team[125] pattern.

> The Product Owner has more to do than a single person can handle well
>
> Therefore
>
> Create a Product Owner Team, led by the Chief Product Owner, whose members together carry out product ownership.

To talk with the developers without ambiguity, understanding the needs and requirements of a diverse crowd of stakeholders to take the decision and directions, they will need an event of clarification that anticipates the Product Backlog Refinement[126]: the MetaScrum Pattern.

---

[125]https://sites.google.com/a/scrumplop.org/published-patterns/product-organization-pattern-language/product-owner-team

[126]http://scrumbook.org/value-stream/product-backlog/refined-product-backlog.html

MetaScrum

> Scrum Teams are in place, but legacy management structures' direction (or the threat of interference) causes confusion about the locus of control over product content and direction.
>
> Therefore
>
> Create a MetaScrum as a forum where the entire enterprise can align behind the Product Owners' backlogs at every level of Scrum in the organization.

MetaScrum is the event that anticipates understanding the business needs and gets clarity for the Product Owner Team. MetaScrum is the place where the beliefs that will drive prioritization are formed.

Who should attend the MetaScrum? Would developers be present? What's the difference with the Product Backlog Refinement, then? In my experience, a good ratio between technical people and business people is 20/80, symmetrically between Refinement and MetaScrum, like a sort of yin and yang[127].

- MetaScrum: 80% of the participants are from business and 20% from development (usually few representatives from the team)
- Refinement: 80% of the participants are the developers and 20% from business (usually the PO Team and a few key stakeholders if necessary)

A MetaScrum aims to create Product Backlog Items that are Good Enough to be discussed during a Product Backlog Refinement with the Developers. In my experience, introducing the MetaScrum creates two natural clarity levels between Product Backlog Items.

---

[127]https://en.wikipedia.org/wiki/Yin_and_yang

Therefore, I used the term *Good Enough* (or just *Good*) to differentiate these items from the *Ready* concept introduced in the Scrum Guide and detailed in the Definition of Ready[128] Pattern.

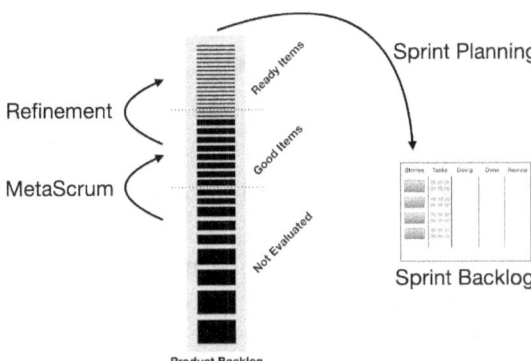

To facilitate MetaScrum events in clarifying the PBI and maintaining a high level of participation, I experimented with the following techniques (valid as well for Product Backlog Refinement).

Triple Nickel

This approach is inspired by the Triple Nickels in Retrospectives[129]. My adaptation aims to clarify the most straightforward PBI quickly, involving everybody only for the more complex requirements.

I organized a circle of "Pods," trying to have a diverse composition. For example, with business stakeholders and two teams, I created Pods of three people with one developer from each team and one stakeholder. Depending on the context, you'll figure it out. The general principle is diversity, so don't create only a pod of developers and a pod of business people. The Chief Product Owner remains outside the Pods, moving from one to another when requested.

[128]http://scrumbook.org/value-stream/product-backlog/definition-of-ready.html
[129]https://gscokart.wordpress.com/2013/02/02/triple-nickels-in-retrospectives/

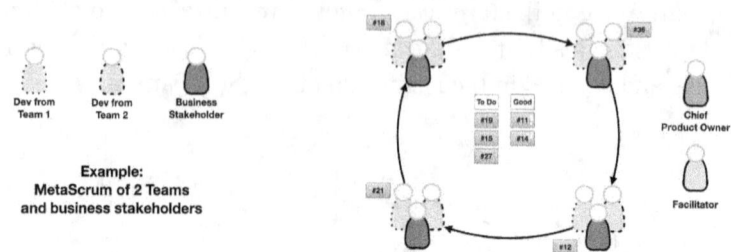

Identify the PBIs to discuss with a token (I often write the ID of the PBI from the software tool on a sticky note) and put them in the center of the table. Each pod pulls one item, reads it on the software tool, and discusses it. They ask themselves questions about the meaning of the item and collect the answers to these questions as acceptance criteria if they know it or as an unresolved question if they don't know it. After a time-box of 10 or 15 minutes, every pod passes the item to the next pod through the circle. If a pod considers a PBI clear enough, they mark it with a green dot. Depending on the number of pods, an item is "Good" (or Ready, if you use this technique during a Product Backlog Refinement) when it has two or three green dots. If a Pod receives an item without any green dot that has already been discussed, they call the Chief Product Owner to clarify the unresolved questions. If needed, the facilitation stops to discuss the critical item altogether. In this way, the easily defined items get through the process without necessarily involving everybody, speeding up the clarification process.

PRODUCT BACKLOG REFINEMENT

- Just as anybody, this is the event that takes time to learn. This team started doing it all together and then decided to do it sending a representative.
- Useful facilitation technique: Triple Nickels Retrospective adapted to Refinement.
- We sit in a circle, including the PO, working in pairs. Each pair pick up a story, append with post-its pieces of information, comments, and questions and pass it to the next pair. If a pair agree that the story is ready, they apply a Green Label. After one full round, the story with more than 3 green labels are called ready, and the PO clarify the remaining stories.

This work is licensed under a Creative Commons Attribution-ShareAlike 4.0 International License.

Case Study By
Paolo Sammicheli

Product Backlog Refinement - Sisma Case Study

1-2-4-All

This technique, popularized by the Liberating Structure[130] community, aims to engage everyone simultaneously in generating questions, ideas, and suggestions. It consists of four time-boxes, as follows:

- **Alone**. Everybody reads the PBI and reflects on it
- **Pairs**. Everybody discusses with another person which elements need to be clarified and specified
- **Four**. Pair of Pairs put the questions they discussed together
- **All**. Each group of four, in turn, asks one question from their list, and the answers are noted in the PBI.

The original format time-box, coming from brainstorming and not from Agile Events, proposes one minute for Alone, two minutes per Pair, four minutes for groups of Four, and five minutes for the ALL. I found this time box too short, so I used the following:

---

[130]https://www.liberatingstructures.com/1-1-2-4-all/

- **Alone**: 1 minute
- **Pairs**: 5 minutes
- **Four**: 10 minutes
- **All**: as needed, within the total event time-box

I recommend experimenting with the time box duration since it depends on the context and cannot be generalized.

Value Poker

This technique aims to facilitate a rich conversation about the value of alternatives. Depending on the situation, it might be alternative features of a product, competing projects, alternative niche markets or use cases, etc.

A mix of different approaches inspires this technique; at the moment I am writing this chapter, I couldn't find another source facilitating it the same way I do it, so it might be a naive way I adapted over time. However, the Excel templates for this technique are available in the Download Section[131] of my website.

The technique starts with a stakeholder spreadsheet containing the list of features and a budget to spend on them. Then, every stakeholder is requested to spend their budget entirely, which is calculated by multiplying the number of options by 30. We have ten features in the example, so the budget is 300; if we had twelve features, it would have been 360.

---

[131]https://paolo.sammiche.li/download

VALUE POKER

			BUDGET	300		LEGEND	
Area	**Feature**	**Value**	TOTAL	0		0	No Value
Area 1	Feature 1		LEFTOVER	300		10	Very Low Value
	Feature 2	0				20	Low Value
	Feature 3	10				30	Average Value
Area 2	Feature 4	20				40	High Value
	Feature 5	30				50	Very High Value
	Feature 6	40					
	Feature 7	50					
Area x	Feature 8						
	Feature 9						
	Feature 10						

I usually send this file to each stakeholder and ask them to spend their budget entirely buying the Features with amounts ranging from 0 to 50. Then, when I have the files from everybody, I merge them in the "Aggregated VPoker.xlsx" file, and I schedule a meeting with all the stakeholders.

VALUE POKER

Area	**Feature**	**SH1**	**SH2**	**SH3**	**SH4**	**SH5**	**TOT**	NOTES	**SH1**	**300**
Area 1	Feature 1	20	10	20	30	20	100		SH2	300
	Feature 2	50	40	50	50	50	240		SH3	300
	Feature 3	50	50	50	40	50	240	Priority is NOT obtained	SH4	300
Area 2	Feature 4	20	40	20	30	20	130	ordering by this column but	SH5	300
	Feature 5	20	10	10	10	30	80	using techniques like		
	Feature 6	20	10	10	10	20	70	Moscow, Kano, etc., and with		
	Feature 7	20	50	30	30	20	150	the information from the		
Area x	Feature 8	10	10	50	20	10	100	conversation.		
	Feature 9	50	40	20	30	30	170			
	Feature 10	40	40	40	50	50	220			

At the beginning of this Value Poker meeting, I show the aggregated file (I avoid showing it before to avoid side conversations outside the meeting), and I ask them questions for each feature. If there are opposite values (like somebody said "Very High Value" and somebody else "Very Low Value"), I ask to share pieces of information (or facts) that support this evaluation. I don't try to make them converge on a single evaluation but share as much information as possible. I bring a note taker with me to speed up this process, often the SM of a team.

After reviewing all the features, we close the event, highlighting that the final prioritization will be determined by comparing the value of each element with the effort and using other product management techniques to have a holistic view of the business value.

The benefit of this technique is that it provides a numerical result and a rich set of evidence and facts. In addition, not making the stakeholders converge on a single vote speed up the process and makes it very useful when you find conflicting stakeholders and strong personalities.

Alternative/Similar approaches on this topic you might want to explore are:

- Buy-a-Feature[132]
- 100 Points Method[133]
- The Product Tree Prioritization Framework[134]

Sprint Planning

When you have multiple teams, Sprint Planning might be long and tedious. With Hardware teams, I successfully implemented a naive pattern that I called "Buffet Planning." It took place in a large room, to which chairs had been removed, with a large table of paper strips containing a Product Backlog Item. The teams were asked to behave according to the rules that we consider polite at an elegant buffet in Italy. In that situation, you cannot take too little food because it would give the idea of not liking the kitchen. What is taken must be entirely eaten since it is impolite to leave leftovers.

---

[132]https://medium.com/left-travel/product-prioritization-buy-a-feature-b5e0caeb25e5
[133]https://www.visual-paradigm.com/scrum/scrum-100-points-method/
[134]https://lazaroibanez.com/the-product-tree-prioritization-framework-d7ab0beff99c

Buffet Planning

- We behave like a real buffet: you can't take too little, because it would not be polite, but you can't take too much because you have to eat whatever you take.
- Very energetic meeting where discussions took place spontaneously; a managed chaos.
- It takes around one hour of discussions for Sprint Planning 1 (what to do). At the end of the hour every team shares with the others what they selected and the CPO checks the table to see if there are high priority items still there. In that (very rare) case, teams are asked to volunteer to replace something they have with the remaining high priority item.

This work is licensed under a Creative Commons Attribution-ShareAlike 4.0 International License.

Case Study By
Paolo Sammicheli

Scaled Sprint Planning - Vimar Case Study

The event begins with the Chief Product Owner proposing Sprint's goal and illustrating PBI's ordering in the table. The Scrum Master showed the Sprint calendar with holidays, meetings, or scheduled leaves. Then the teams were asked to pull the paper strips from the table and freely converse about what needed to be done and who was the best Team to do that job. We observed the formation of different groups of people animatedly discussing with one or more Product Backlog Items in hand, a real creative and focused chaos.

The Chief Product Owner alternated between conversations, making himself available to answer questions. After the first hour, the Scrum Master call the break to make the various teams share which PBI they had already taken and vote if more time was needed. Before the end of this collective moment, the Chief Product Owner ensured no urgent residual PBI was on the table and asked questions. Prioritization changes were often driven by unresolved dependencies or strategies to develop more quickly. Usually, after an additional hour of Sprint Planning, in which the teams worked separately to discuss the solution and create the tasks, the first developers were already starting to work on the priority item.

BUFFET PLANNING

- We behave like a real buffet: you can't take too little, because it would not be polite, but you can't take too much because you have to eat whatever you take.

- A very energetic meeting where discussions took place spontaneously; a managed chaos.

- No chairs in the room: the result is short and concise discussions.

This work is licensed under a Creative Commons Attribution-ShareAlike 4.0 International License.

Case Study By
Paolo Sammicheli

Scaled Sprint Planning - Sisma Case Study

Sprint Review

Even in a Scaled environment with multiple teams, I try to maintain the Sprint Review as a single event. This constraint forces the teams to integrate the development into the increment before the end of the Sprint and drives good technical discipline. It will also increase the chance of key stakeholders attending if this is only one event for multiple teams.

SPRINT REVIEW

- The review covers increments from pre-sale to shipment and one-site installation, using 3D models, diagrams, simulations, photos, and videos.

- The production site area is next door, most of the time, the conversation continues in front of the real machine, if it's not already shipped.

- With Scrum for Hardware "shipped" means that the product it's on a truck on the way to the customer! It's not easy like with software! 😉

This work is licensed under a Creative Commons Attribution-ShareAlike 4.0 International License.

Case Study By
Paolo Sammichelli

Scaled Sprint Review - Sisma Case Study

In the Sisma Case Study, the CEO was often attending the Sprint Review, and we used different techniques depending on the state of development in which the deliverable was. For increments still in design, animated 3D models showed the element's functionality. When the prototype parts were available, they were brought to the Review and physically inspected. For the completed machines and therefore already shipped, they were filmed with a smartphone at the last testing before the shipment.

Deployment / Review

- Teams have dedicated rooms where integrate and test, very often during the Sprint, the products.
- These rooms usually are used also for the Sprint Review, so they all have projectors and foldable chairs to accomodate guests.
- The different products are installed in several movable panels. They can also be taken into the team room during the Sprint for convenience.

This work is licensed under a Creative Commons Attribution-ShareAlike 4.0 International License.

Case Study By
Paolo Sammicheli

Scaled Sprint Review - Vimar Case Study

Also, in the Vimar Case Study, it has been necessary to modify the rooms to work, creating a laboratory dedicated to frequent product integration and Sprint Reviews. The Marostica headquarters' teams were provided ample space by removing a dividing wall between two rooms over the weekend. This way, communication between these teams during the Sprint was significantly simplified, and continuous integration was implemented.

Skills and Teams

As we previously discussed, you must have a modular architecture to reduce time-to-market developing different parts of the product in parallel.

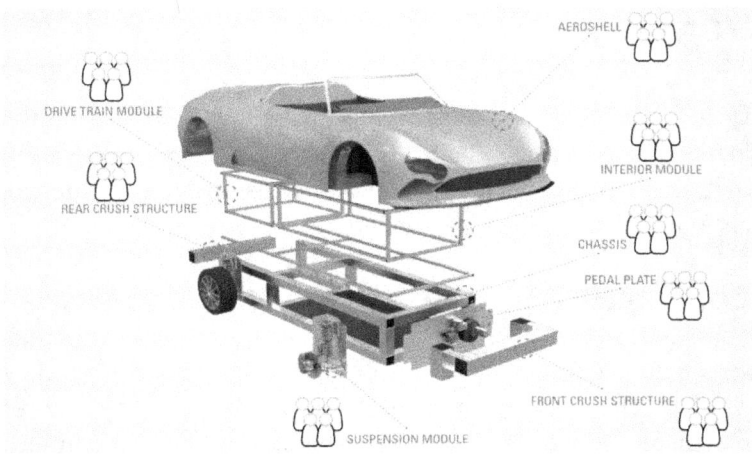

This kind of division would create a fragile organization when a team could only work on a single part. Using the skill matrix tool, you need to assess the ability of the teams to work on different parts, aiming to have Teams like the **Delta** in the following picture.

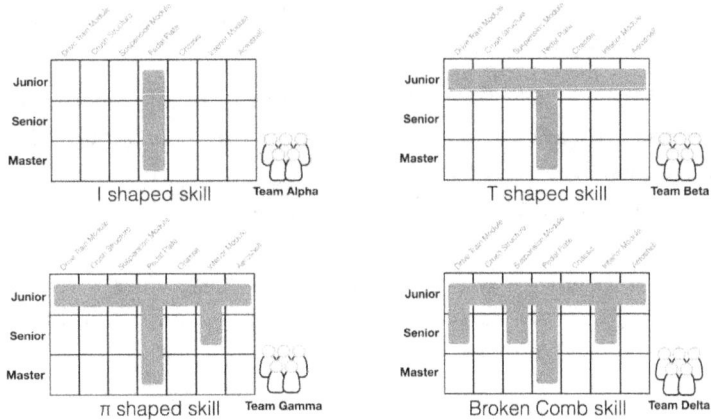

Once again: Skillset is the ultimate constraint when you design organizations. Therefore, it's critical to highlight the bottlenecks in terms of skillsets and to implement all the possible measures to enable the organization to keep learning continuously.

Vendors

Up to this point, we discussed Scaling in terms of adding capabilities in the form of teams. In Hardware, though, you will inevitably meet the need to include vendors in your development. How to negotiate an Agile collaboration with vendors?

Contracts: Win-Lose vs Win-Win Lose-Lose

Traditional contracts in vendor-client relationships are typically win-lose. They are fixed in scope, time, and cost, and any changes require renegotiations, leading to delays and cost overruns. In such contracts, the vendor "wins" by delivering the least possible value within the fixed constraints, while the client "loses" if changes or unexpected issues arise. On the other hand, if the client successfully forces the vendor to deliver more than initially agreed, they will "win" while the vendor will "lose" because of shrinking revenue.

These win-lose contracts are antithetical to the principles of agility, where adaptation and continuous improvement are core values.

In contrast, Agile encourages a win-win, lose-lose approach to contracts. These are based on mutual trust, collaboration, and shared risk. They allow for changes in scope during the project, with time and cost as variables. The parties agree to share profits and losses based on the success or failure of the project. While these contracts require greater trust and openness, they can lead to better outcomes, as both parties are incentivized to deliver the highest possible value.

Agile Contracts

An innovative type of contract, known as the "Money for Nothing, Change for Free" contract[135], merges the best of both worlds.

---

[135]Money For Nothing and Your Change for Free: https://www.scruminc.com/agile-2008-money-for-nothing-2/

Coined by Jeff Sutherland, this model offers the customer the right to terminate the remainder of the contract if they believe the value delivered by the vendor is enough, effectively getting "money for nothing." The "change for free" clause allows the customer to substitute features of the same or lesser value, providing flexibility and adaptability.

This type of contract incentivizes the vendor to over-deliver since the early termination of the contract can result in reduced revenue. At the same time, it ensures that the customer always has the flexibility to adapt to changes, reflecting the agile principle of welcoming change. To learn more about Agile Contracts, you can watch this interesting video[136] from Scrum Inc. and this article from Lean-Agile Procurement about the Agile Contracts Manifesto[137].

Dealing with Vendors with eXtreme Manufacturing

In eXtreme Manufacturing[138], the iterative and incremental framework for manufacturing developed by Joe Justice within the Wikispeed project, the tenth principle talks about Vendors and partnerships. The concept expressed is very interesting. On one side, it says to treat vendors more like partners and involve them in the design decisions and make suggestions:

> Ask them to deliver a particular set of performance characteristics instead of an engineering specification. "Do you have a transmission suitable for a 100hp motor?" not "Here is our design for a transmission, can you build it?" Why should you wait months for a supplier to build a device to your specifications when they have a device

---

[136]https://www.scruminc.com/agile-contracts/
[137]https://www.lean-agile-procurement.com/blog-1/2022/2/20/agile-contracts-the-only-template-youll-ever-need
[138]The complete description of eXtreme Manufacturing is available later.

that will satisfy your needs already in the catalog or in stock?

On the other hand, the approach is to first decouple from the vendor using the Wrapper Pattern:

> Once each third-party part is wrapped in a known interface, you can iterate between suppliers and in-house prototypes or volume parts at a meager cost. The only marginal cost is that of changing the wrapper itself.

I found this approach of "trusting but not depending on them" quite inspiring.

Integrating Vendor with Scrum

When I worked with Vimar Spa, helping them to start the Scrum Teams to develop the Smart Home platform, we had the problem that the initial configuration was scaled, counting dozens of people, that at some point extended to 3 different sites. To mitigate this, I used the Scrum of Scrums Pattern, previously discussed. Multiple parts of the platform, though, were developed externally. So I needed to incorporate the Vendors into the Team of Teams.

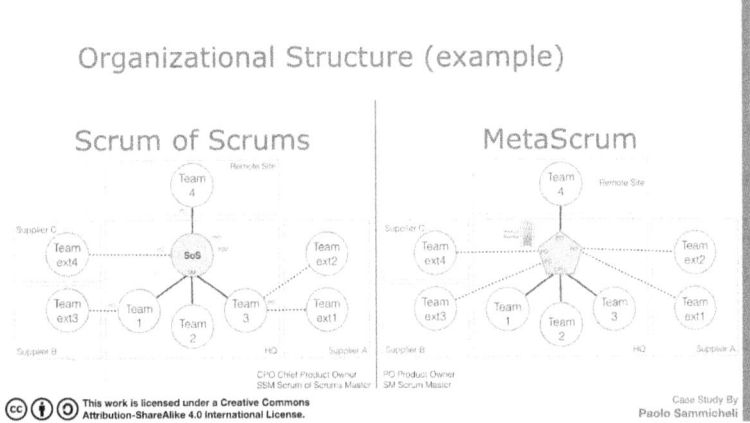

Scaled Organizational Structure - Vimar Case Study

I asked the Chief Product Owner to treat the Vendors like teams, part of the Team of Teams. Each Vendor had a Product Backlog of deliverables prioritized by a Product Owner. The contract was a simple time-and-material, so we removed the need to have all the specifications upfront. The people prioritizing each vendor's Product Backlog, which we still called Product Owners, weren't people external to the development but senior developers sitting on a team. Their job was to prioritize the external work to mitigate the dependencies with the Team of Teams' high-level backlog, test the frequent releases from vendors, and integrate the release into the entire platform with the help of the other developers.

We used the approach of having only one Sprint Review, so everything developed internally and externally needed to be integrated within the Sprint.

Deployment / Review

- Teams have dedicated rooms where integrate and test, very often during the Sprint, the products.
- These rooms usually are used also for the Sprint Review, so they all have projectors and foldable chairs to accomodate guests.
- The different products are installed in several movable panels. They can also be taken into the team room during the Sprint for convenience.

This work is licensed under a Creative Commons Attribution-ShareAlike 4.0 International License.

Case Study By
Paolo Sammicheli

Scaled Sprint Review - Vimar Case Study

The Product Owners for the external vendors were always representing them at the Scaled Sprint Planning, even though sometimes a few developers from the Vendors were joining the Sprint Planning as well. At that time, hybrid work with remote and in-house people collaboration wasn't as popular among hardware companies as it is today after the COVID-19 pandemic.

Buffet Planning

- We behave like a real buffet: you can't take too little, because it would not be polite, but you can't take too much because you have to eat whatever you take.
- Very energetic meeting where discussions took place spontaneously; a managed chaos.
- It takes around one hour of discussions for Sprint Planning 1 (what to do). At the end of the hour every team shares with the others what they selected and the CPO checks the table to see if there are high priority items still there. In that (very rare) case, teams are asked to volunteer to replace something they have with the remaining high priority item.

This work is licensed under a Creative Commons Attribution-ShareAlike 4.0 International License.

Case Study By
Paolo Sammicheli

Scaled Sprint Planning - Vimar Case Study

In other undisclosed implementations of Scrum in Hardware I've worked on after 2020, I implemented the Buffet Planning pattern on a virtual board, like Miro[139], and all the vendors attended every Scrum event.

Lean-Agile Procurement

Sometimes, you will need to buy something big or select which vendor to choose at the beginning. This is the topic that is traditionally managed by Procurement and can be addressed with Mirko Kleiner's Lean-Agile Procurement[140] approach. Lean Agile Procurement applies lean and agile principles with a process that involves classic product techniques to streamline and optimize procurement as rapidly as possible. It is particularly effective in complex procurements where collaboration between diverse teams and individuals is vital for success. The approach is relatively new, disrupting traditional practices and offering a simpler, more engaging, and more efficient process.

Key Techniques of Lean-Agile Procurement

The essence of LAP lies in several key techniques that make it unique:

- **Lean Procurement Canvas**: These are visual representations that allow teams to understand a product's strategic goals at a glance.
- **Definition of product**: Concise and compelling summary of a product or service, similar to an elevator pitch.
- **Big room evaluation**: bringing potential partners together for live, collaborative assessment sessions with short feedback loops.

---

[139]https://miro.com
[140]https://www.lean-agile-procurement.com

- **Constant collaboration**: The approach emphasizes frequent cooperation between various teams with diverse skills.

Lean-Agile Procurement Canvas

The Lean-Agile Procurement Canvas, inspired by Ash Maurya's Lean Canvas and Alexander Osterwalder's Business Model Canvas, is an integral part of the LAP approach. It presents the evaluation in a structured, comparable format, first focusing on the highest risks. It serves as an agile contract, eliminating the need for extensive legal documentation.

Lean Procurement Canvas

On the right-hand side, we have all about the company that is evaluating a new partner, which is analyzed on the left-hand side. The main question is, can they both together achieve the main goals in the middle? The lean procurement canvas is easy and gives the evaluation a comparable structure that follows the highest risks first.

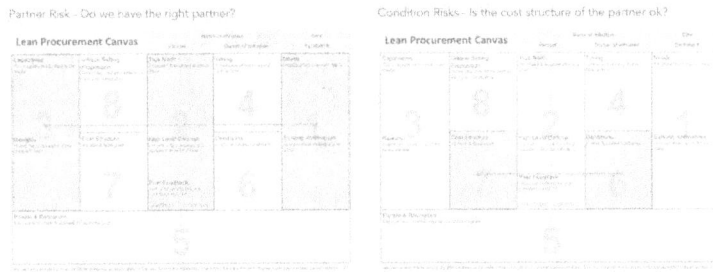

Risk 1: Do we have the right partner?-If not stop here   Risk 2: Are the conditions matching?-If not stop here

Lean Procurement Canvas risks 1-2

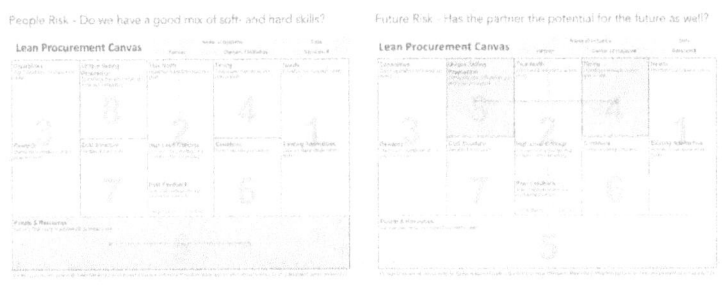

Risk 3: Will the team fit and do the job?-If not stop here   Risk 4: Has the partner the potential for the future?-If not stop here

Lean Procurement Canvas risks 3-4

Lean-Agile Procurement Process

The Lean-Agile Procurement process can be broken down into four principal steps, as described in the following picture.

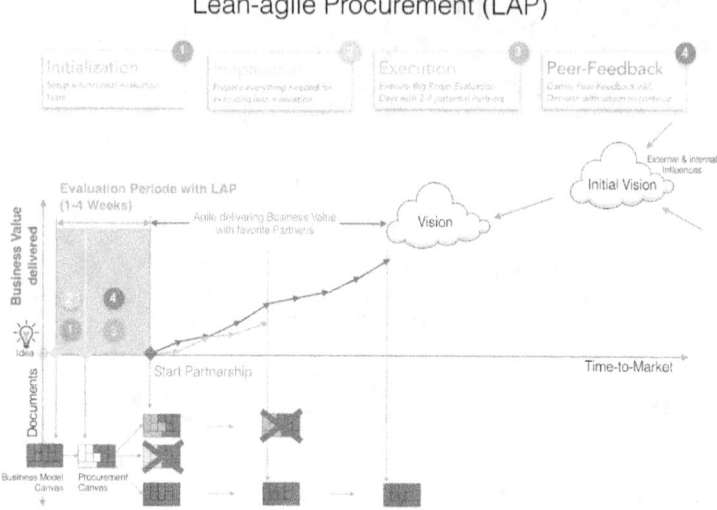

1. **Initialization**: Establish a cross-functional procurement team that includes individuals who will work with the new partner.
2. **Customer Needs Design**: Define high-level needs and prepare relevant information. Share this with potential partners who should come to the big room evaluation with their teams.
3. **Big Room Evaluation Days and Peer-Feedback/Decision**: Organize evaluation days with potential partners, collaboratively working out the Lean Procurement Canvas. The goal is to complete the canvas and gather peer feedback.
4. **Start Agile Delivery**: Begin agile delivery with the chosen partner, using the Lean Procurement Canvas as the key instrument in partner management.

Who Can Benefit from LAP?

Lean Agile Procurement is suitable for various professionals, including executives, procurement managers, delivery heads, scrum masters, and human resource managers. It benefits organizations already implementing agile principles or those transitioning towards a lean-agile approach. LAP has been successfully applied in both the private and public sectors.

By rethinking traditional procurement processes through Lean-Agile Procurement, organizations can achieve significant improvements in efficiency, cost-effectiveness, and speed to market, transforming procurement from a cost center into a strategic advantage.

In a Scrum for Hardware development scenario, Lean-Agile Procurement is the right approach to bring the vendors that will later be part of the Team of Teams.

Managing Multiple Projects

As the Author
I want to discuss how to manage projects with Scrum
So that non-product-centric organizations can understand how to be agile.

Products or Projects?

It's common knowledge that Scrum underscores the concept of a 'Product.' Various Scrum terms underscore this perspective - the Product Backlog, the Product Owner, and more. The Product Backlog is a prioritized list of features that could be included in the final product, managed by the Product Owner. The Scrum approach, therefore, orbits around one product rather than projects, like is stated in the 2020 Scrum Guide:

> The Product Goal is the long-term objective for the Scrum Team. They must fulfill (or abandon) one objective before taking on the next.

In stark contrast, traditional methods, often seen in the Project Management Institute's (PMI) methodologies, emphasize projects. Evidently, even the institute's name itself reflects this focus. Project Management principles hinge on initiating, planning, executing, controlling, and closing the work of a team to achieve specific goals within a defined timeline. Let's delve into definitions. An excellent 'Product' definition comes from the Scrum Guide:

A product is a vehicle to deliver value. It has a clear
boundary, known stakeholders, and well-defined users
or customers. A product could be a service, a physical
product, or something more abstract.

On the other hand, a 'Project' is:

a temporary endeavor designed to produce a unique
product, service, or result with a defined beginning and
end.

Today's digital age is pivoting towards a product-oriented approach.
More organizations are leaving behind the rigid project framework,
which mandates defined scope, time, and cost parameters at the
onset. These pre-determined guidelines are increasingly rare in a
fast-paced, evolving market environment. Proof of this shift is the
#noprojects movement, which you can explore at noprojects.org[141],
advocating for a transition away from project-based organizations.

However, it's crucial to note that this shift isn't universal or one-
size-fits-all. For instance, if you're a hardware developer contracted
to build specific parts for a client's product, your focus is on the
project - the stipulated part's specifications.

Interestingly, it's possible to use the Scrum framework within a
project management framework, even though Scrum is inherently
product-centric. However, if the rest of the development follows a
traditional, waterfall, project-based approach, incorporating Scrum
will not miraculously enhance overall development performance.
The results depend on the broader development landscape and the
unique context of each endeavor. This chapter will show how to use
Scrum in a project-centric market.

---

[141]https://noprojects.org

Embracing Minimum Viable Bureaucracy

If Scrum is utilized within a project management framework, the primary objective is to streamline and minimize bureaucracy. This goal often necessitates discerning between self-inflicted, unnecessary paperwork and legitimate deliverables manifested in documents.

Self-imposed paperwork often emerges from well-intentioned procedures that have morphed into bureaucratic redundancies. To eliminate these, we must scrutinize the original, positive intentions driving these processes and explore alternative ways of implementing them without generating unnecessary work.

Furthermore, all deliverables should be reflected as product backlog items, keeping them tied to the product's progress and visible to all stakeholders. This approach keeps everyone focused on delivering value rather than simply producing paperwork.

While creating the initial product backlog, a helpful tool to manage deliverables can be a mind map. This visual representation, displaying all the deliverables in a hierarchical structure, can clarify their relationship and priority. The mind map guides the team to focus on value delivery while keeping bureaucratic requirements bare minimum. I coached teams in multiple markets, like construction and automotive, that found it helpful to share this representation with their counterparts with real-time online boards such as Miro[142] or Mural[143]:

---

[142]https://miro.com
[143]https://mural.co

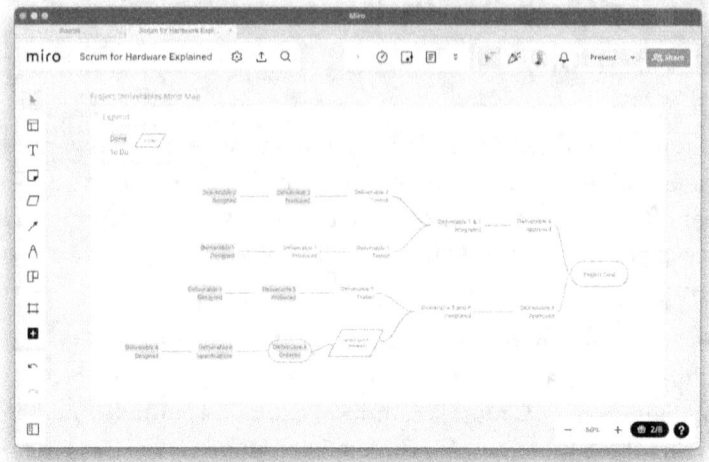

Project Deliverable Mind Map

A visual and shared understanding between all the counterparts represents the essence of the Minimum Viable Bureaucracy approach. Another helpful approach would be to use the Enabling Specification[144] pattern.

> Unexplored requirements cause unpleasant surprises.
>
> Therefore
>
> The Product Owner should deliver Enabling Specifications as a sign that they have done due diligence in exploring the requirements space.

An Enabling Specification is a specification rich enough that someone reasonably skilled in the discipline can implement a solution without substantial subsequent clarification with people outside the Scrum Team. The phrase enabling specification is a term of law applied as a US standard for valid patents:

---

[144]https://sites.google.com/a/scrumplop.org/published-patterns/value-stream/product-backlog/enabling-specification

"A patent specification is enabling if it allows a person of ordinary skill in the art to practice the invention without undue experimentation."[145]

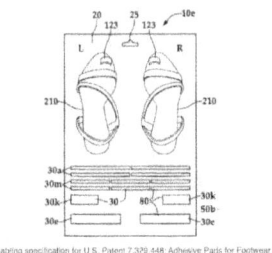

Enabling specification for U.S. Patent 7,329,448: Adhesive Pads for Footwear

Enabling Specification from "A Scrum Book by J. Sutherland, J. Coplien"

An Enabling Specification is typically composed of no more than a few pages and contains designs, schema, and diagrams to make everything clear without extended writing. More information can be found in Scrum Inc's article "Enabling Specifications: The Key to Building Agile Systems[146]."

Scrum in Engineering and Construction projects

Let's explore how Net Engineering, an Italian mobility engineering firm that works on big international projects across Europe, Asia, and Africa, adopted Scrum throughout their entire organization. They utilized it to manage a diverse portfolio of projects, including roads, bridges, tunnels, railroads, high-speed train tracks, train stations, bus stations, parking areas, cycling lanes, and more.

---

[145]Jay Dratler, Jr. and Stephen M. McJohn. "Obtaining Patent Rights." in Intellectual Property Law: Commercial, Creative, and Industrial Property, Volume 1, 1991, New York, NY: Law Journal Press.

[146]https://www.scruminc.com/enabling-specifications-key-to-building/

Engineering and Construction Increments - Net Engineering Case Study

Why Scrum

Motivated by a desire to manage increasing project complexities better, empower personnel, and foster team spirit, Net Engineering chose to adopt Scrum on a company-wide scale.

Why Agile and Scrum

Scrum helps us to solve some criticalities:

✸ To manage complexity   ✸ To put people at the center

! To empower people on   ✦ To foster the team spirit
  decision making

This work is licensed under a Creative Commons Attribution-ShareAlike 4.0 International License. Copyright - Net Engineering

Why Agile and Scrum - Net Engineering Case Study

Projects in this sector are exceptionally challenging. Characterized by three levels of maturity, as dictated by Italian public construction regulations: Preliminary project, final project, executive project, and construction site management. The entire period, from preliminary project to construction site management, can span several years. Large construction projects, such as extensive routes of high-speed trains, may even last more than a decade. Each team's objective was to maximize completed work, thus adopting the Kanban principle of "Stop Starting, Start Finishing!"

Scrum Board

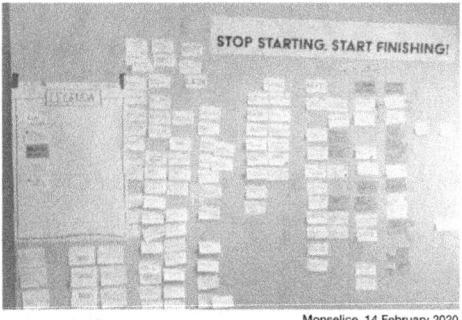

Monselice, 14 February 2020

Pilot Team Scrum Board - Net Engineering Case Study

Cross-functionality and Cross Team Coordination

The issue of cross-functionality among teams was another problem tackled. The vast array of skills (or disciplines) needed to execute these projects can be overwhelming, and the learning curve is steep. In such contexts, experts such as water engineers or seismologists need over a decade of experience to qualify as "senior." The Scrum concept of T-Shaped skills is only attainable after considerable practice.

Net Engineering structured itself using Scrum@Scale's Team of Teams approach to address these challenges. They implemented the Scaled Daily Scrum, the Metascrum, and the Scaled Retrospective as scaled events.

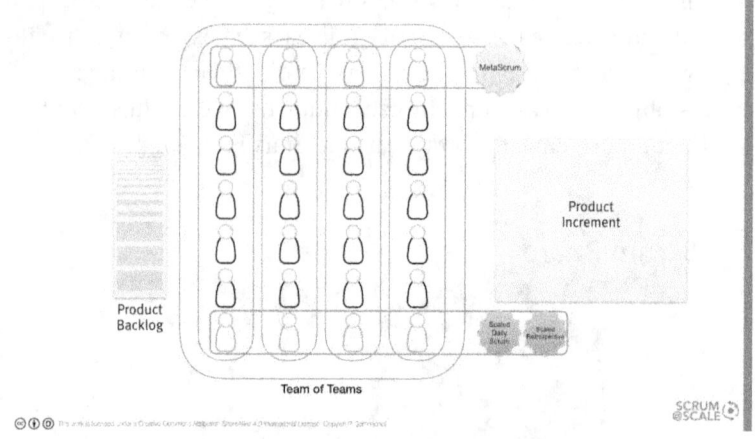

Scrum Scaled Events - Net Engineering Case Study

This organizational restructuring also impacted the company's structure. They transitioned from a siloed hierarchical organization to a network of teams guided by a Management Team composed of the CEO, the CFO, the Scrum of Scrums Master, and the Chief Product Owner[147]. This approach allowed for more fluid communication between different disciplines, devoid of hierarchical barriers.

---

[147]At the moment of writing, two years after the case study publication, they further divided themselves into two Value Streams (splitting between Engineering and Architecture projects), with each one a Chief Product Owner and dedicated scrum teams.

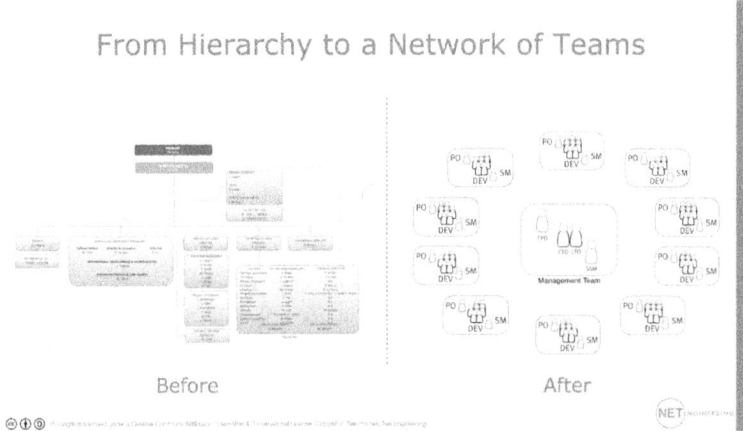

NET ENGINEERING

Organizational change - Net Engineering Case Study

Communities of practice were established to bolster technical competencies and foster a better understanding of different disciplines. These aimed to address cross-team design decisions and enhance skills.

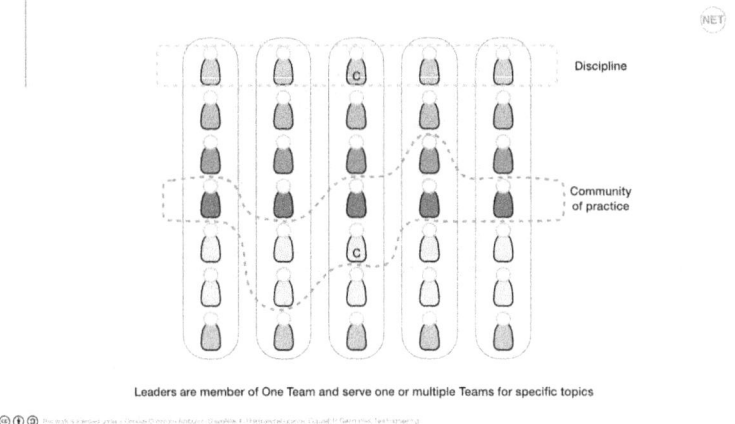

Leaders are member of One Team and serve one or multiple Teams for specific topics

Disciplines and Communities of Practice - Net Engineering Case Study

An interruption buffer was implemented across all teams to manage disruptions and facilitate prompt work transfers between teams.

Offloading work items: Interruption Buffer

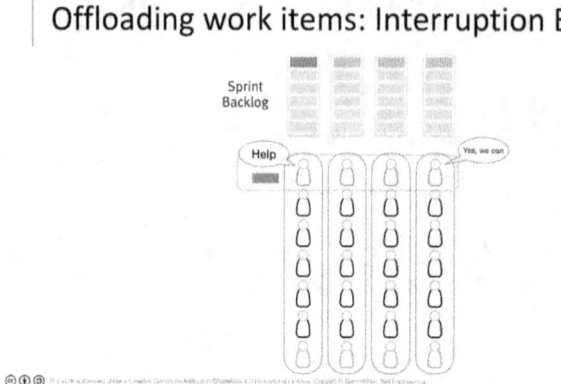

Interruption buffer - Net Engineering Case Study

In cases where an impediment could not be resolved by altering team backlogs, such issues were escalated directly to the daily Scrum of the Management Team since the Scrum of Scrum Master is part of it.

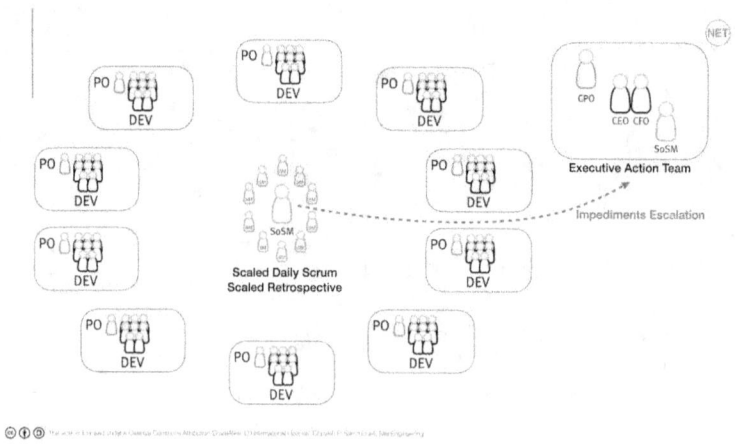

Impediment escalation - Net Engineering Case Study

Project Portfolio Management

To manage their extensive project portfolio, they adhered to Scrum@Scale principles and implemented a single Product Backlog for the entire organization, named "Enterprise Backlog." This was initiated during the formation of the first pilot team before having all teams in place.

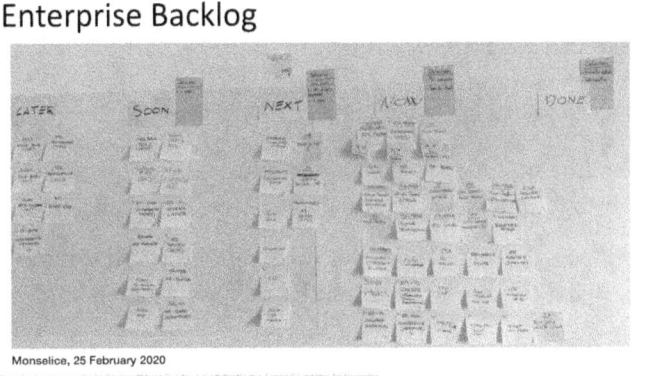

Enterprise Backlog, first draft - Net Engineering Case Study

Two years later, when we published this case study, the Enterprise Backlog was maintained on a Trello board, accessible to all Product Owners.

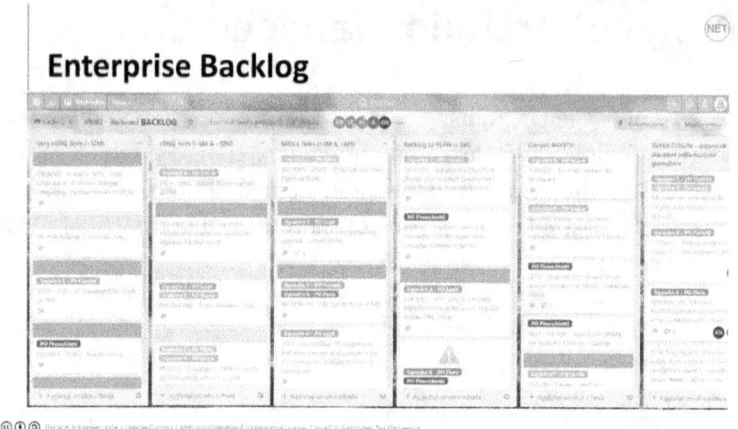

Enterprise Backlog, two years after - Net Engineering Case Study

Color coding was used to indicate various data points, such as ownership by a Product Owner, known dependencies, impediments, etc.

Sprint Reviews played a crucial role, particularly during the pandemic. Being fully remote posed the risk of losing sight of project progress.

When the case study was published, Sprint Reviews were conducted remotely due to the pandemic. However, as restrictions eased, they transitioned to in-person and hybrid formats. Timings and agendas were predetermined, enabling each team to invite stakeholders to their respective time slots. Various techniques, including Renders, Designs, and Videos, were tested to gather early feedback.

Remote Sprint Reviews

Remote Sprint Reviews - Net Engineering Case Study

Scrum and BIM: Synergistic Benefits

The Building Information Modeling (BIM)[148] is a digital represen-tation of the physical and functional characteristics of a facility. It serves as a digital twin[149] to foster shared knowledge and become a reliable basis of information for decisions during its life-cycle from inception onward.

Fortuitously, they had the opportunity to implement Scrum in the organization while the BIM process was concurrently advancing and expanding.

These two frameworks, Scrum and BIM, complement each other remarkably well. They share common principles and mutually enhance their benefits. Both:

- Advocate for knowledge-sharing: Both frameworks empha-size information sharing, encouraging transparency and bet-ter decision-making.

---

[148]https://en.wikipedia.org/wiki/Building_information_modeling
[149]https://en.wikipedia.org/wiki/Digital_twin

- Encourage holistic understanding: Rather than confining team members to their specialist contributions, both Scrum and BIM empower them to understand the bigger picture, fostering a more integrated approach to problem-solving and project progression.
- Promote stepping out of comfort zones: both Scrum and BIM provide frameworks that challenge team members to move beyond their comfort zones, leading to growth, innovation, and increased productivity.

Scrum + BIM benefits

We had the chance to implement Scrum in our organization while our BIM process was improving and spreading.
These two frameworks have a lot to share and they foster each other, as both:

- are based on knowledge-sharing

- let the members of the teams see the big picture and not just their own speciality contributions, and to go out of their comfort zone.

- BIM helps also to reduce Scrum risk of some teams isolation.

This work is licensed under a Creative Commons Attribution-ShareAlike 4.0 International License. Copyright: Gianni Ezzat, Net Engineering

Scrum and BIM benefits - Net Engineering Case Study

Additionally, BIM can effectively mitigate one of the potential risks associated with Scrum – the possible isolation of certain teams. By fostering a more integrated approach to project planning and execution, BIM encourages inter-team collaboration and communication, reducing the likelihood of team isolation.

Benefits and Points of Attention

Net Engineering's application of Scrum to their management of engineering and construction projects yielded significant benefits while revealing areas requiring further attention.

Among the many benefits were the rapid identification and elimination of roadblocks, the streamlined onboarding process for new hires, and the alleviation of feelings of isolation and distance during remote work periods.

Scrum's strength lies in its ability to flag potential issues early, enabling swift decision-making in dynamic project environments. Careful refinement of the product backlog facilitated improved future activity planning.

Additionally, Scrum simplified team management, making it more manageable to oversee ten teams rather than a hundred individuals. The stability of the Scrum Team composition and the consistent continuity of personnel on projects boosted project effectiveness and team satisfaction. Furthermore, Scrum's team-centric philosophy encouraged individual members to focus on collective goals, promoting a feedback culture.

Despite these benefits, there were areas requiring attention. The limited number of roles within Scrum necessitates a mindset shift among our Product Owners, mainly a focus on return on investment and identification of team development opportunities. The dual role of Scrum Masters and Product Owners in technical delivery also presents challenges. Almost everyone serving as a Scrum Master and Product Owner has unique technical skills, so balancing development perspectives with leadership challenges is essential, regardless of the methodology adopted.

Also, complexities arise when projects extend across multiple teams, but the continued use of Building Information Modeling has proved beneficial in such situations. Another focus area is the enhancement of Scrum events. While team members desire more opportunities to share, discuss, and seek advice, Scrum is designed to facilitate these activities. As a management team, they are committed to fostering team independence and self-sufficiency, leading to the most effective implementation of Scrum.

Next steps

- Solve Points of Attention
- Extend the Scrum adoption internationally
- Keep improving

This work is licensed under a Creative Commons Attribution ShareAlike 4.0 International License. Copyright © Sam Nitzan, Net Engineering

Final slide - Net Engineering Case Study

In Production

As the Author
I want to show how to extend Scrum in Production
So that readers can improve their agility in the entire company.

The machine that makes the machine

During the 2016 Tesla shareholder meeting[150], Elon Musk presented a groundbreaking concept: the 'Machine that makes the Machine.' He emphasized that the crux of manufacturing lies not in the product itself but in the factory that creates it.

2016 Tesla's Shareholding Meeting - Screenshot from tesla.com

The concept revolves around viewing the factory as a meticulously designed product rather than a random assembly of various components purchased from different sources. This perspective echoes

---

[150]Video at https://www.tesla.com/2016shareholdermeeting, from 02:20:30 to 02:28:28

the approach Tesla takes with its vehicles. Instead of assembling a car from a selection of pre-manufactured parts, Tesla designs the vehicle according to its specific requirements, manufacturing the necessary components in-house or in collaboration with suppliers. The Model S, for instance, contains almost no components found in other vehicles.

Musk argued that the potential for improvement in this 'machine-making machine' is far greater than the potential for improvement in the car itself, perhaps by a factor of 10 or more. After spending considerable time on the production floor, he arrived at this under-standing, observing the manufacturing process first-hand.

Thinking in terms of Physics' First Principles, the output of a production facility is a function of three parameters: volume, den-sity, and velocity. Musk pointed out that a factory's volumetric density of 'useful' to 'non-useful' components is surprisingly low, perhaps only two or three percent. Therefore, a substantial scope for improvement exists.

The velocity of vehicle production is another aspect with potential for improvement. Advanced car factories worldwide produce a car every 25 seconds, which initially seems fast. However, considering that the length of a car, including a buffer space, is approximately five meters, the exit velocity of vehicles from the factory is merely 0.2 meters per second, not much faster than a tortoise. Musk argued that factories should be able to produce cars at least at walking speed.

Designing a factory like an advanced computer system can yield significant improvements. By applying principles from computer design, such as focusing on clock speed and data transfer, the production process's efficiency can be dramatically enhanced.

Shifting design resources from improving motor technology, power electronics, or batteries to optimizing the factory has the potential for significant gains. Instead of struggling for fractional improve-ments in the product, the same engineering effort can yield substantial improvements in production.

To implement this strategy, Musk advocates educating engineers about the potential for improvement. Many engineers tend to concentrate on the product itself, unaware of the possibilities of improving the production process. By dispelling these misconceptions and redirecting their efforts toward the 'machine that builds the machine,' significant advancements can be made in manufacturing efficiency. This strategy followed actual actions, like the Grohmann Engineering [151] and Perbix Machine Company[152] acquisitions.

Teslaspeed

In April 2022, Germany's vice-chancellor Robert Habeck called for unprecedented measures to decrease the country's reliance on Russian gas and counter the Kremlin's energy blackmail as Russia's war on Ukraine enters its third month. To describe the need for rapid action, he coined the term "Teslaspeed."

> The vice-chancellor previously called for new infrastructure at "Tesla speeds." The American carmaker recently stunned Germans by erecting and opening a new Gigafactory close to Berlin in a mere two years.[153]

Tesla's Gigafactory

The Gigafactory concept represents a radical shift in battery production and electric vehicle (EV) manufacturing. Envisioned as enormous facilities covering millions of square feet, Gigafactories centralize the entire battery production process, from raw material

---

[151]Tesla acquires Grohmann Engineering to boost production: https://techcrunch.com/2016/11/08/tesla-acquires-grohmann-engineering-to-boost-production/

[152]Tesla just bought an automation company to help it build the factory of the future: https://www.businessinsider.com/tesla-buys-perbix-facts-details-2017-11

[153]https://www.euractiv.com/section/energy/news/germanys-habeck-we-have-to-try-the-unrealistic-to-break-free-from-russian-gas/

acquisition to finished packs. This integration aims to scale production and reduce costs, making EVs affordable for the mass market. Key elements of the Gigafactory include[154]:

- **Vertical Integration**: By controlling everything from raw material extraction to finished products, dependencies on external suppliers are reduced, and quality control is enhanced.
- **Advanced Automation**: Utilizing automation and robotics, the Gigafactory optimizes efficiency and accuracy in manufacturing.
- **Research and Development**: These facilities also function as centers for innovation in battery technology, driving advancements in energy storage.
- **Sustainable Energy**: Gigafactories emphasize sustainability by utilizing renewable energy sources like solar panels and wind turbines, reducing carbon footprints.

Musk refers to the Gigafactory as "the machine that builds the machine," underlining its pivotal role in Tesla's mission to produce electric vehicles on a mass scale. Tesla's scale, affordability, and sustainability goals would be unattainable without these facilities. Gigafactories emphasize quality control and large-scale production of high-performance batteries by encapsulating self-sufficiency and vertical integration.

In conclusion, the Gigafactory concept revolutionizes battery production and emphasizes self-sufficiency, vertical integration, and sustainability. It is crucial in accelerating the global transition to sustainable energy and transportation, symbolizing innovation and human ingenuity.

To get an idea of Giga Berlin, you can watch this spectacular YouTube Video[155]:

---

[154]Source: Gigafactory: The Machine That Builds the Machine - Aaron Smet https://medium.com/the-tesla-digest/gigafactory-elon-musks-vision-and-the-machine-that-builds-the-machine-af9c80b7f65e

[155]https://www.youtube.com/watch?v=7-4yOx1CnXE

Flying Through Giga Berlin - Tesla's YouTube Channel

Production Line Agile Development

The evolution of manufacturing continues to inspire and challenge the way we think about production. One concept that stands out in modern manufacturing practice is Production Line Agile Development.

Cellular Assembly Line: The Cornerstone of Agility

The cellular manufacturing[156] process is a just-in-time and Lean Manufacturing subfield. This approach divides production into "cells," each responsible for a specific task. As a product moves from cell to cell, often in a U-shaped design, each station accomplishes a part of the manufacturing process.

---

[156]https://en.wikipedia.org/wiki/Cellular_manufacturing

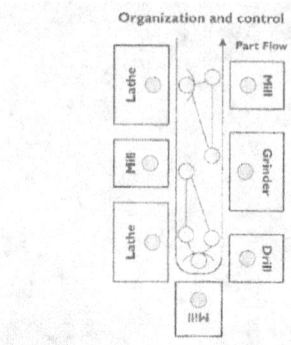

Figure 8-4. U-shaped one-piece flow cell

Figure 8-4 from The Toyota Way - Erinwott, via Wikimedia Commons

This structure allows for incredible flexibility and rapid adjustments to scaling, design changes, or even complete product overhauls. Efficiency, quality, and waste reduction are some hallmarks of cellular manufacturing, with one-piece-flow cells often termed "the ultimate in lean production."

Elon Musk's Philosophy: Treating the Production Line as a Product

Elon Musk has taken the concept of the cellular assembly line a step further by treating the production line itself as a product. This innovative perspective shifts focus from merely producing a product to optimizing the way the product is produced. It recognizes the production line as a complex, evolving entity ripe for innovation and improvement, just like any other product.

Starting the Assembly Line Team Early

To achieve genuine agility in the manufacturing process, starting the team responsible for the assembly line is essential as soon as the product's general architecture is drafted. This timing ensures that both the machine and the machine that makes the machine are developed in tandem, feeding insights and improvements into one another.

Parallel Working and Iterations: Breaking Down Phases

Traditional manufacturing often involves a linear sequence of design and industrialization. However, the Production Line Agile Development promotes parallel working between the two teams responsible for these phases. Allowing iterations and continuous collaboration ensures that the design is adaptable and that the industrialization process aligns perfectly with the evolving product. This parallel working approach dissolves the barriers between the designing and industrialization phases, encouraging continuous feedback and adaptation.

Realizing the Vision: A Dynamic Collaboration

The true success of the Production Line Agile Development lies in the dynamic collaboration between product and production line teams. This approach creates an environment where innovation flourishes by initiating the assembly line's development just after the product's general architecture is formed and encouraging iterations between the two teams, forming a Team of Teams.

This collaboration goes beyond simple coordination; it creates a symbiotic relationship where insights from one team directly fuel the other's development. The process is iterative, flexible, and responsive, aligning seamlessly with the agile principles of adaptability and continuous improvement. One example is the Tesla Cybertruck shape, which is optimized for production[157].

> The one thing which gives the Cybertruck its looks is the angular overall shape and the basic lines of the body panels. It seems this is because (according to Tesla) the material is so hard that it cannot be stamped into curves

---

[157]Source: Why does the Tesla Cybertruck look like that? https://wisconsinmetaltech.com/tesla-cybertruck/

as it would break the stamping press. This can be taken with a pinch of salt, but it does explain the looks.

Therefore, Tesla devised a 'new' manufacturing process whereby they used laser cutting to make the panels. This also means that Tesla has been able to speed up and simplify the manufacturing process for the Cybertruck and keep the pricing low (relatively).

The Cybertruck at its 2019 unveiling - via Wikimedia Commons

Tesla's Agile New Product Introduction

Let's dissect the dynamic nature of Tesla's manufacturing philosophy with this conversation[158] between Lars Strandridder, host of the BestInTesla[159] YouTube Channel, and Joe Justice, founder of the Wikispeed project and former Tesla employee.

[158]https://youtu.be/Pk4Ygmd8fLc?t=2257
[159]https://www.youtube.com/@BestInTESLA

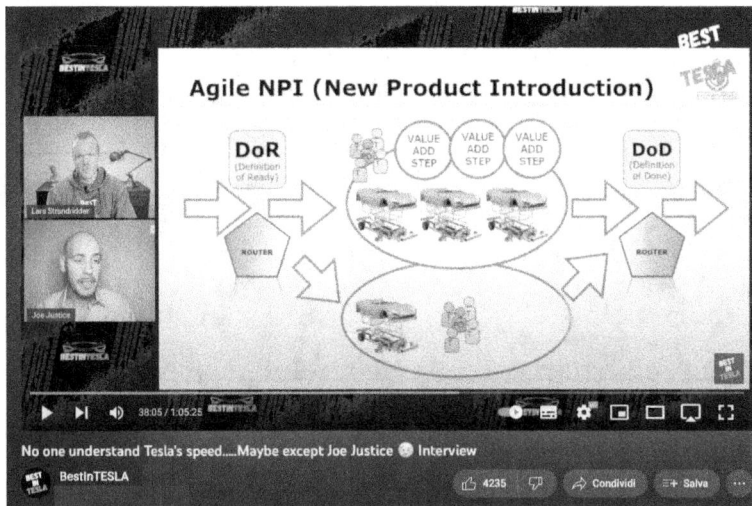

Interview to Joe Justice - BestInTESLA YouTube Channel

A Living Cell Approach to Production

Rather than relying on a conventional production line, Joe explains that Tesla uses a system akin to the living cells in a body. It's an analogy that encapsulates a process where things move as needed and where nutrition flows organically. This living cell system at Tesla defies traditional structure, focusing on efficiency and flexibility.

In Tesla's production cells, various value-added steps occur, such as installing heat pumps, sealing, and riveting. An optical machine-learning system, such as autopilot, plays the role of quality control, ensuring that parts are ready for the next stage. This decision is visualized through a heat map, where green means go.

Radical Innovation and Continuous Improvement

What sets Tesla's agile system apart is its constant drive for innovation. Joe shares the fascinating detail that radical innovation often occurs right on the factory floor, sometimes even in a parking lot under the shade. Small, cross-functional teams work on improvements, such as increasing the efficiency of a heat pump by 20%.

These innovations can be seamlessly integrated into the production line through routers that act like train track switches. If an improved part passes the definition of done, it is immediately incorporated into the product, and someone buying a Tesla may get an upgraded part.

The Production Ramp: A Never-Ending Journey

The conversation between Lars and Joe also unveils the complexity of Tesla's production ramp. It's a system where pilot lines and main lines coexist, working on different versions of parts, always aiming to improve.

In one day, various versions of each part are made, each attempting to become the new best. The production ramp never ends; before it reaches 100%, a new and better innovation takes over, constantly pushing the boundaries of efficiency and effectiveness.

Production Line development with Scrum

In July 2019, I helped Pietro Fiorentini Spa introduce Scrum in Production in their facility at Desenzano, on the beautiful Garda Lake. The selected product was the Production Line for a New Gas Pressure Regulator for civil use.

Context

The selected Scrum Team Product was the **Production Line** of a New Gas Pressure Regulator.

The New Gas Pressure Regulator (in the picture) was develop by another Team in another site and started before the production line.

This work is licensed under a Creative Commons Attribution-ShareAlike 4.0 International License. Copied from Pietro Fiorentini Gas Tech Demo Ambarabà Project.

Scrum Team Product - Pietro Fiorentini Case Study

The development of the actual product that you see in the picture started a few weeks before this story. The Production Line Scrum Team has been formed using the same approach described before:

- Value Stream Mapping of the Production Line
- Skill Mapping and Skill Matrix
- Team Composition to include all the necessary skills
- Team Lift Off

The newly formed team included developers from different departments: Tooling, Maintenance, and Logistics. During the Lift Off, they named themselves "the Rolling Scrums."

Pilot Team formed: theRollingScrums

- The existing KPO served the team as Scrum Master
- Cross functional team with representatives from: Tooling department, Maintenance and Logistics

Pilot Team - Pietro Fiorentini Case Study

The space dedicated to the Team's work was located directly in production, in the area that would host the assembly line once it was finished. They had full autonomy on how to organize the space.

Scrum Team Room

Scrum Team space - Pietro Fiorentini Case Study

In this ample space, the team had everything necessary to design, prototype, build, and test the cells composing the assembly line. When we started adopting Scrum, the developers already used a method called Lean 3P to design and construct new assembly lines. So they lent me a book with which I tried to understand the fundamental components of the method and find the points of contact with Scrum.

Incremental development with Lean 3P

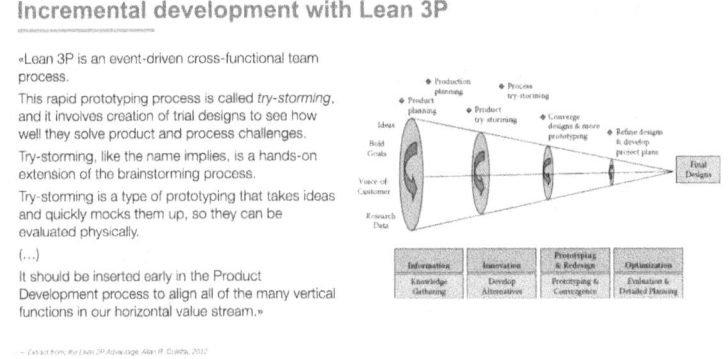

«Lean 3P is an event-driven cross-functional team process.

This rapid prototyping process is called *try-storming*, and it involves creation of trial designs to see how well they solve product and process challenges.

Try-storming, like the name implies, is a hands-on extension of the brainstorming process.

Try-storming is a type of prototyping that takes ideas and quickly mocks them up, so they can be evaluated physically.

(...)

It should be inserted early in the Product Development process to align all of the many vertical functions in our horizontal value stream.»

— Extract from the Lean 3P Advantage, Alan R. Coletta, 2012

Lean 3P - Pietro Fiorentini Case Study

It is an incremental development method in which, with a cross-functional workgroup, prototypes are frequently shown to representatives of the various functional offices, with an approach called try-storming.

The revealing sentence for me said: "3P should be included early in the development cycle to align the different vertical functions in our horizontal value stream". "Great!" I thought, "The method is perfectly compatible with Scrum!". The essential difference is that Scrum, by creating a stable cross-functional team and establishing roles, also introduces an organizational change, which Lean 3P does not require. Everything else looked very similar, so I incorporated Lean 3P into Scrum, just like the various other engineering practices.

Architectural Fishbone served as User Story Mapping

©①② This work is licensed under a Creative Commons Attribution-ShareAlike 4.0 International License. Copyright Pietro Fiorentini S.p.a. ©2015 Jacopo Romei, Andrea Provaglio.

Architectural Fishbone - Pietro Fiorentini Case Study

I asked the Team: "If I weren't here, how would you create the to-do list?" They showed me a fishbone diagram that showed the assembly sequence of the parts of the product. "Is it the operators' action to assemble a gas pressure regulator? In Scrum, we use User Story Mapping, which visualizes the user tasks; it's the same principle. Let's use this fishbone to create our User Stories! ". We started writing the stories: "The operator wants to insert the valve into the regulator," "The operator wants to screw the valve into the regulator," and so on. We used color coding to show the confidence about components' maturity of the other team developing the Gas Pressure Regulator:

- Green - parts that were considered relatively stable.
- Red - parts that were not stable enough and subject to further changes.

To simplify the upcoming changes in the cells with red components, they implemented Design Patterns, such as adapters and wrappers, following the approach of Agile Architecture and Contract First Design, described later in the Extreme Manufacturing chapter.

Once we had the first set of stories, I heard the Team saying things like, "We still have to do the 'x10' of this cell while we can do the 'x50' of this other one because it's similar to the old regulator". I asked what these x10, x50, and x250 were.

Lean 3P and Scrum

• Lean 3P incremental level served as User Story's Acceptance Criteria.

• Very smooth adoption since the team members were familiar with the approach from the beginning.

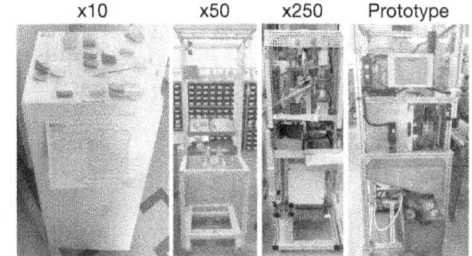

ⓒⓘⓞ

Lean 3P incremental levels - Pietro Fiorentini Case Study

They explained to me that it was the prototyping level. The first level, x10, was made of cardboard and allowed the discussion of the footprint, the input of materials, the output, and the production flow for each cell. The second level, called x50, was made of wood and made it possible to discuss ergonomics, management of supplies, etc. The x250 model was made of aluminum and housed working parts, such as electric screwdrivers, which could be used by the team for testing, certainly not by production operators. Just after the x250, a cell prototype was created. With minimum training, operators could use it to produce small quantities and test the process. Finally, the mass production model was built, with all the ergonomics and efficiency characteristics. "What do these numbers mean in practice?" I asked curiously. "Compared to an abstract design, these models allow you to learn five times as much, so the numbers represent this, the amount of feedback and learning that multiplies each time by a factor of five. This approach is called

TryStorming. We design by trying". "Brilliant," I said, "In Scrum, we have acceptance criteria for User Stories. It is the same principle. Let's use this numbering to indicate the level of prototyping of each user story". As team members saw their practices incorporated easily into Scrum, enthusiasm grew.

Once the first Product Backlog was created, we proceeded with Sprint Planning and designing the Sprint Board. Since the team dealt with the new product development and other secondary activities, such as maintaining old products, we implemented several Scrum Patterns from the beginning.

Sprint Board

- Including everything: Features, Bugs, Chore, Interruptions and Kaizen.
- Scrum Patterns implemented:
  - Interruption Buffer
  - Scrumming the Scrum
  - Yesterday's Weather
  - Swarming

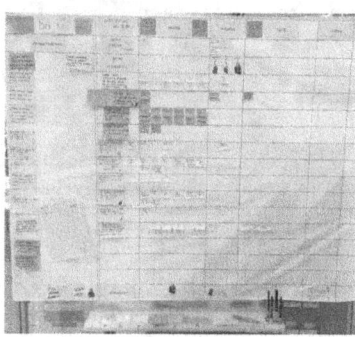

Sprint Board - Pietro Fiorentini Case Study

Therefore, the board's first horizontal line was used for the improvements from the retrospective (Scrumming the Scrum). The second line contained the interruption buffer (Illegitimus Non-Interruptus), and from the third onwards, the Sprint Backlog stories. In addition to highlighting the Sprint number and the date of the next Sprint Review, the board's title showed the average velocity of the last three Sprints (Yesterday's Weather).

3D Printing to shorten feedback

Rapid Prototyping - Pietro Fiorentini Case Study

As already described several times, the approach to incremental development to shorten the feedback loop was already a fundamental element of the company culture. For example, the group designing the gas pressure regulator produced prototypes of the model in plastic, using a 3D printer, to allow the "RollingScrums" to have physical components to start working.

Sprint Review

Sprint Review - Pietro Fiorentini Case Study

After the first couple of Sprints, the team was confident enough, and we invited various Stakeholders to the Sprint Reviews, including the Plant Manager. The product demos were very interactive and engaging, allowing participants to touch the different solutions. To overcome the excessive noise of the environment due to the production lines bordering the Scrum Team's space, we equipped ourselves with a microphone and amplifier so that all participants could hear the explanation of the demonstration. A second microphone was passed between participants for questions, considerations, and feedback.

Benefits

- Increased know-how sharing across the Team
- Distributed Leadership
- Effectiveness together with Efficiency
- Responding to change — with a stable team, the time required to change priorities or to start a new project moved from weeks to hours
- The Sprint Review structured the feedback in a single moment, increasing stakeholders alignment and reducing risks
- Easier planning with a Single Scrum Board that contains everything: new implementations, fixes, interruptions

Benefits - Pietro Fiorentini Case Study

Among the practical benefits, Andrea Aganetti, representing Pietro Fiorentini Spa, mentioned that forming a Scrum Team allows a more homogeneous distribution of Know-How, with consequent team spirit, involvement, and motivation. Scrum also introduces a concept of distributed leadership, which makes the staff more responsible. Having prioritized Product Backlogs allowed them to incorporate new needs and priority changes with an effort of a few hours instead of the weeks it took with traditional project management. The characteristic of always prioritizing higher-value activities led Pietro Fiorentini's leadership in this transformation process to improve the work's effectiveness while maintaining attention to the efficiency of Lean Manufacturing. Furthermore, Scrum events' flow provided a regular cadence much appreciated by the stakeholders, who found the Sprint Reviews to be the place to structure the feedback and align with the progress made.

Finally, compared to the past approach, the Sprint Board, complete with the " Interruptions Pattern" and "Scrumming the Scrum," has allowed us to bring all the activities of the Team to a single board, whether they are development, maintenance, and improvement, simplifying management and increasing transparency.

Points of Attention

- Better to involve the main stakeholders from the beginning so they enter in the right mindset of cadence and early regular feedback.
- Initial team composition needs to be taken into consideration, since later changes may impact on the performance and the morale of the team
- Management commitment is essential to allow team members to be fully dedicated to the SCRUM team

Points of Attention - Pietro Fiorentini Case Study

As points of attention, it should be noted that involving all Stakeholders in the introductory training sessions on the method is crucial. Also, consider team formation carefully since a later variation of members causes delays, impediments, and decreased morale. In this, the involvement and participation of Management is essential.

Engineering Practices

As the Author
I want to show the engineering practices
So that Scrum Developer understands how to iterate
with hardware quickly.

One of the most challenging things for many Scrum teams is to create an **increment** at the end of every Sprint. We want feedback and learn as much as possible from it. What if the hardware product is technically very complex? How to build an Increment in just one or two weeks?

Software teams use a set of engineering practices, known under the name of eXtreme Programming[160], like Test Driven Development (TDD), Pair Programming, and Continuous Integration, but those are contextual to Software development. What if you have to deal with complex tangible products?

Extreme Manufacturing is a set of principles created by Joe Justice during the WIKISPEED project. Those principles have been published by Peter Stevens[161], a Certified Scrum Trainer who lives in Zurich, Switzerland.

In this chapter, you will find the Wikispeed story; in this way, you'll understand the naive context where those practices originated. After the Wikispeed story, you will find a copy of the original article Extreme Manufacturing Explained[162] enriched with photos, links, lexicon improvements, and additional notes.

---

[160]https://en.wikipedia.org/wiki/Extreme_programming
[161]https://saat-network.ch/about-saat-network/about-peter-stevens-cst/
[162]http://www.scrum-breakfast.com/2013/06/extreme-manufacturing-explained.html

Wikispeed

Wikispeed[163] is an automotive open-source project with a modular design car founded by Joe Justice and headquartered in Seattle, Washington. Wikispeed competed in the Progressive Automotive X Prize competition in 2010 and won 10th place in the mainstream class, with a hundred other cars competing, often from big companies and universities.

Introducing Joe Justice

In 2008, Joe Justice was a software consultant living in Denver, Colorado. He worked for Avanade, a large software company and a joint venture between Microsoft and Accenture, developing interesting software projects for large businesses. At the beginning of the year, he received a phone call: an Accenture employee was forming the team for a new project for the Bill & Melinda Gates Foundation, founded by the American magnate and patron of Microsoft and considered the wealthiest man in the world. Joe's curriculum seemed highly suitable for that project: besides learning about the .NET development environment and Microsoft Sharepoint, the two leading technologies of the project, Joe also had experience with Scrum, the Agile development method that the Gates Foundation had decided to adopt for all new projects. Scrum's experienced staff was scarce in Accenture, so they offered Joe to fly to Seattle every Sunday and return home every Thursday night for the following months. The idea of working with the Bill & Melinda Gates Foundation was inspiring, and Joe did not hesitate to accept; he would be the Scrum Master of the Avanade team at the Foundation and would teach Scrum to the entire organization. Joe knew Scrum well; he had used it since his first job in Denver as a developer. He considered it the only serious way to develop software in a business context.

---

[163]https://en.wikipedia.org/wiki/Wikispeed

Joe had become interested in computer science since he was a kid. Being the youngest of six children, Joe was intrigued by the games of his four sisters and his older brother, John. In particular, that strange object – a computer called Commodore Vic 20 allowing them to watch new worlds and live exciting adventures on his TV thanks to some tapes – fascinated him. When he was about to go to university, Joe chose the faculty of computer science, emulating his older brother, who had already graduated and was enjoying the economic boom[164] in the late 90s, earning good money. Joe had received a scholarship offer from a prestigious university and was enthusiastic about starting this journey. However, something went wrong: shortly before starting the courses, he received a letter from the university stating that the scholarship was supposed to be allocated to the Hispanic minority and there had been a mistake. He was not qualified to access it. Joe, an adolescent and inexperienced person then, did not think to seek advice from a lawyer; he consulted with his school secretary. Thanks to the student placement officer's knowledge, he obtained a scholarship from the University of Wyoming. It was an alternative far below his expectations, but Joe was OK with it and decided to accept.

Ai, a young Japanese student, attended classes on the same campus, where she also held a language and culture course about her country, as required by the international scholarship that brought her to the US.

Joe made no secret of his passion for Japanese culture with his friends: he had received it from his mother, who had spent her childhood in Japan following her father, a prominent US Army General, on a mission to the island. Joe's roommate, who knew about this, met Ai in class and told him immediately: "You must know my Japanese teacher; she is definitely your type. I'm sure you'll like her". "I don't like older women," Joe replied. "She is our age! Trust me, you must know her".

It was love at first sight for Joe, and as soon as he left university, he

---

[164]https://en.wikipedia.org/wiki/Dot-com_bubble

asked her to marry him. They were young, newly graduated, and with little money. They decided to get married and celebrate their wedding in Hawaii so that friends and families from Japan and the United States could join them easily to celebrate all together. They then spend their honeymoon exploring Hawaii, renting several cars along the road.

One morning, great sports car enthusiast Joe was driving a small convertible on the road to Hana. He felt in heaven, with his young wife sitting by his side and a gentle breeze coming from the forest and refreshing his face. Suddenly, despite feeling so well with a smile spread from ear to ear, he saw that paradise slowly blurs in front of him. "If every single individual of the 7 billion populating the planet would like to enjoy this same pleasure – he thought – the forest could no longer exist. It would be replaced by a bare clearing devastated by acid rain, and the air would smell of exhaust gas."

Since he was a child, Joe naturally developed a solid ecological sensitivity. He still remembers that when he was 4 or 5, he prevented his older sister from killing a grasshopper with ether, which she needed for science school research. In an attempt to save the insect, Little Joe cried and threw such a tantrum that he lost his senses by hyperventilation, alarming the whole family.

And now, the only thought of a devastating forest made him feel almost physically distressed. Such stomach-burning feeling wiped that smile off his face for the rest of the trip, and that disturbing image began to haunt him even at night. He felt guilty, as if he was doing something wrong or unfair. During this trip, Joe fully understood the ecological meaning of "unsustainable." This thought was disconcerting, and he felt he had to react and do something. But what exactly?

The Challenge

The XPrize Foundation is a nonprofit organization based in St. Louis, Missouri, which organizes public competitions to encourage technological innovation. It is a moral institution aiming to identify solutions to complex problems with its initiatives and facilitate financing projects that can benefit humanity in different fields (medical, aerospace, environmental, etc.); in 2008, with sponsorship from Progressive Insurance, the Foundation announced an Automotive XPrize competition with a ten-million-dollar prize. Participants were challenged to build a four-seater eco-friendly vehicle that could be legally registered in the United States, producing less than 200 grams/mile CO_2 equivalent emissions, able to achieve 100 MPGe (100 miles per gallon equivalent of petrol, that is 100 km per 2.8 liters) and that could be manufactured for the mass market. Over one hundred competitors, including individuals, companies, and universities worldwide, participated in the competition.

Wikispeed's Birth

It was immediately clear to Joe that he had to participate in the XPrize. Contending with the challenge of constructing an ecological car would have been the best way to overcome the discomfort during his honeymoon. Unfortunately, although he was a car enthusiast, Joe was utterly new to mechanical expertise. Before that moment, he had not even changed the oil in his car, and he knew the need to learn many things. However, he did not let himself be scared by these initial obstacles and decided to focus on his goal: he placed a large board in his garage and hung a sticky note saying, "Win the XPrize."

How to proceed? Where to start? Joe knew only one method to develop something serious: **Scrum**. He began to apply the "user story splitting" method to his car. Targets were broken down into sub-objectives, thus becoming smaller and more reachable at acceptable times.

Joe wrote the first two objectives on sticky notes: "Build a car that can be registered" and "Build a 100MPG car". Joe recurrently split them into subtasks so that his board was full of sticky notes within one afternoon.

Wikispeed Product Backlog

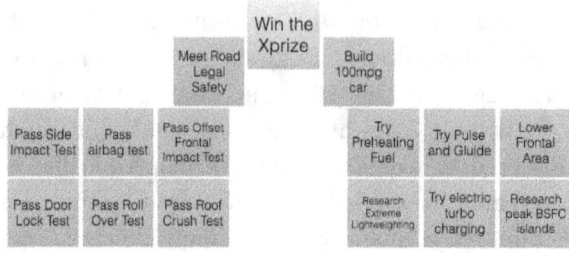

Wikispeed initial Backlog - Courtesy Joe Justice

He knew he could not do it alone, so he began sharing this idea on his blog, telling the world about his experiments, mistakes, and new learnings. He asked specialized communities for help and advice, and people worldwide began to answer, offering suggestions and opinions. Joe replied to anyone who could provide a little support. He updated his followers and asked for further information. Many mechanics, electric technicians, and simple hobbyists began to be interested in the project. Someone even wanted to meet in person "that guy on the internet" who tried to build the most ecological car ever designed, and strangers started arriving to spend the weekend with Joe after flying at their expense over the US. Wikispeed[165] was born: a community of enthusiasts who, like Wikipedia, were developing collaboratively and openly a 100 MPG car to participate in the XPrize competition.

Toward XPrize

In 2010, Joe and his wife moved to Seattle, Washington, for some time. The Bill and Melinda Gates Foundation project had been

---

[165]http://wikispeed.org

going on for two years, and some weekends, instead of going back to Denver, Joe had asked Ai to join him in Seattle. Like any good Japanese, Ai has a vast food culture. The excellent cuisine of the typical restaurants in Seattle, along with the variety of choice of international restaurants, had convinced her that it was worth moving there. Also, Seattle was the headquarters of significant companies, including Amazon, Microsoft, and Starbucks; it seemed an exciting city from different perspectives.

The Wikispeed project was going on quickly: it counted a group of 44 people coming from 4 countries and actively helping Joe. It had a Facebook group[166] with a thousand fans already and a YouTube channel[167] with many followers. After the evaluation phase of the documentation for admission to the competition, Joe and his team started the operation phase, and they built in three months only their first prototype called SGT01, Super Grand Touring 01.

The SuperGT[168] class is a car racing championship in Japan with road cars. They are probably the fastest vehicles that resemble standard cars; better performance is obtained only from cars similar to Formula 1. Joe had always been fascinated by those competitions, and, in his imagination, the car he was planning would have to look as much as possible like a racecar, beautiful and charming. Simultaneously, it had to consume so little to be the most ecological car ever built.

The first simulated tests showed[169] that the car could reach 104MPG on urban cycle and 114MPG on extra-urban cycle: already perfect to win the contest!
Also, weighing only 1300 Lbs. (about 589 Kg), it could go from 0 to 60 miles per hour (nearly 100 Kph) in less than 5 seconds and reach a top speed of 149mph (about 240 Kph). The prototype went like greased lightning! On April 6, during a trial run, Joe ended up

[166]https://www.facebook.com/WIKISPEED/
[167]https://www.youtube.com/user/WIKISPEED
[168]https://en.wikipedia.org/wiki/Super_GT
[169]http://wonderfulworldofwikispeed.blogspot.fr/2010/04/faq.html

colliding with a wall. Luckily, the crash tests carried out on the simulator confirmed very realistic: Joe did not hurt too badly and, with a one-day work and not too much expense for the materials, Wikispeed was as good as new.

On April 12, the team obtained the official confirmation[170] so longed-for by everyone: Wikispeed had been admitted to the final selection, called Shakedown, which was to be held from May 2 to 8, 2010 at the international circuit of Michigan, 100 km west of Detroit and location of the famous NASCAR racing.

It was great news.

The development team at the Bill and Melinda Gates Foundation was also very excited by the idea, and everyone went out of their way to allow Joe to take the necessary vacation to get the business done.

However, finding a specialist mechanic quickly became necessary, as Wikispeed had the Honda Civic engine. If necessary, during the final selection, the team had to be able to intervene without hesitation. Moreover, the race was only less than three weeks away! Joe and his friends published an ad on Craigslist humorously titled "Mechanic/MacGyver (Michigan International Speedway)":

> Team WIKISPEED is competing in the final rounds of the Progressive Automotive X Prize, and we need a fantastic Honda mechanic to support our team at the Michigan International Speedway the week of May 2-8. We are building a prototype car that will go 100 mpg and will retail for under $20k. The challenges we will hit will probably be pretty novel– no repairs are routine on a prototype car. Ideally, the candidate would be willing to work at a reduced rate or gratis since we are a small volunteer team. An attitude similar to the TV show MacGyver's would help.

---

[170]http://wonderfulworldofwikispeed.blogspot.it/2010/04/we-did-it-detroit-here-wikispeed-comes.html

With that single ad, they got an answer from Bryan, a certified technician with experience in Honda engines. In addition to working for free and taking part in the Wikispeed project, Bryan refused some job offers, which were not so abundant in the Detroit area during that crisis period.

Moreover, a certain Todd, owner of a company producing Plexiglas material, offered to help build and install the transparent canopy for free that would protect the pilot in return for the only flight to Seattle.

Finally, Mike, a robotics enthusiast attending a Yahoo-themed forum, showed up unannounced at Joe's garage, where volunteers were working at Wikispeed. No one had ever seen him before, but he spent the whole afternoon working hard and solving some wiring problems that Joe, despite his efforts, had not been able to come to grips with for weeks.

The Big Day

May 5: Eventually, the big day! The entire Wikispeed team is along the Michigan International Speedway – palpable excitement is in the air. The team members did not sleep for three nights to finish the car according to the competition's rules.

Wikispeed Team at 2011 Xprice - Courtesy Joe Justice

Everybody invested time and expertise into the project and felt it as his own. It's Wikispeed's turn.

The jury examines the prototype, and some problems arise. The team does not let this get it down and keeps working: in a few minutes, Wikispeed is disassembled into its main modules (chassis, engine, front dashboard, etc.), and all the participants work in pairs and parallel on the components.

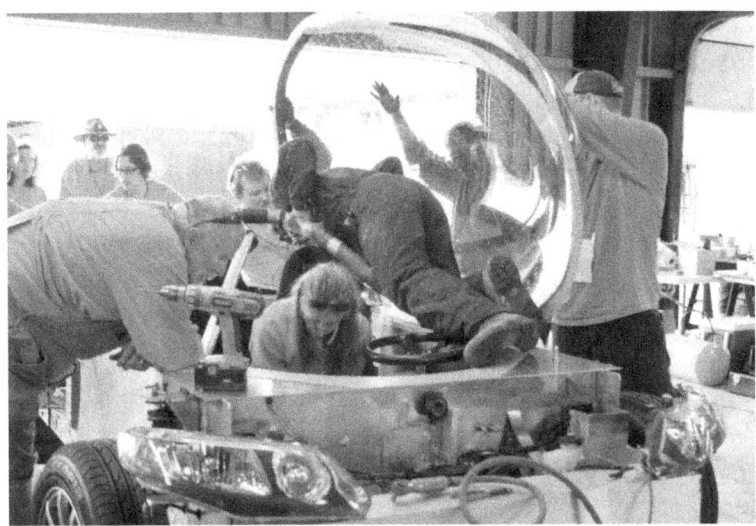

Wikispeed Team working at 2011 Xprice - Courtesy Joe Justice

The jury and rival teams are impressed by the speed and readiness with which the Wikispeed team solves the highlighted problems one by one and congratulate them several times. After finishing the work, the team rolls the car into the designated area for the final inspection. All together, towards glory!

Wikispeed Team before final inspection - Courtesy Joe Justice

Just before the inspection, Joe asks his brother John to help him move the seat belt straps. It was an optional recommendation in the list of change requests, but it seemed simple to do in a few minutes. Lack of sleep and lucidity played their part. Drilling the frame with the drill, Joe accidentally shears an electric cable inside it. Turning to Mary Wilkes, the team's expert electrician, he begged her: "Can you fix it?" Unfortunately, it was impossible in the few minutes left before the final inspection, and the car could not start when the judges arrived. The team appealed to the judges, asking for a little more time to solve the electrical problem by showing that it had just occurred, but the extension was not granted.

However, that was a moment of great disappointment for everyone, compensated by the satisfaction of being positioned tenth on the final ranking, surpassing prestigious and well-funded competitors such as TESLA, TATA Motor, and the Team from Boston MIT.

Wikispeed's SGT01 at XPrice 2011 - Courtesy Joe Justice

More importantly, Wikispeed obtained vast media coverage: the story of Joe and his volunteers appeared on numerous blogs and online magazines, the number of fans continued to grow steadily after the end of the competition and, despite having no victory in the XPrize, the Wikispeed project began to be considered a triumph.

The Ingredients for Success

Sometime later, an article on Fortune[171] listed some elements that had led to the success of Wikispeed, suggesting that firms should consider the following four principles that helped them:

1. Reach out to passionate people

"No matter how many smart people you have at your firm – said the article in Fortune – there are a lot more on the outside. Competitive success hinges upon connecting with others and taking advantage of the knowledge they can bring. So, the benefits of connecting with and bringing together passionate people can be significant." Since the beginning, Wikispeed has used social networks and specialized forums, getting help and suggestions from passionate people worldwide.

2. Keep timelines short

Traditional corporate projects require the creation of two- to five-year strategic plans and detailed blueprints. On the other end of the spectrum, Team Wikispeed works in 7-day cycles, constantly reflecting on different results. What they can do better in the next cycle, and the learning and adaptation cycle is so fast that it allows non-skilled people to achieve very ambitious results quickly.

3. Make the project modular

If you have a monolithic product, it will be very difficult to evolve and improve quickly because the impact of any change will be such as to compel you to review important parts of the entire work. On the opposite, Wikispeed consists of independent modules connected to each other through clear and predefined interfaces. This way, Team Wikispeed manages to improve a single module

---

[171]http://fortune.com/2012/06/18/how-companies-ought-to-train-their-staffers/

with no recourse to the entire work, with the possibility of seeing the results of the changes within the same iteration week.

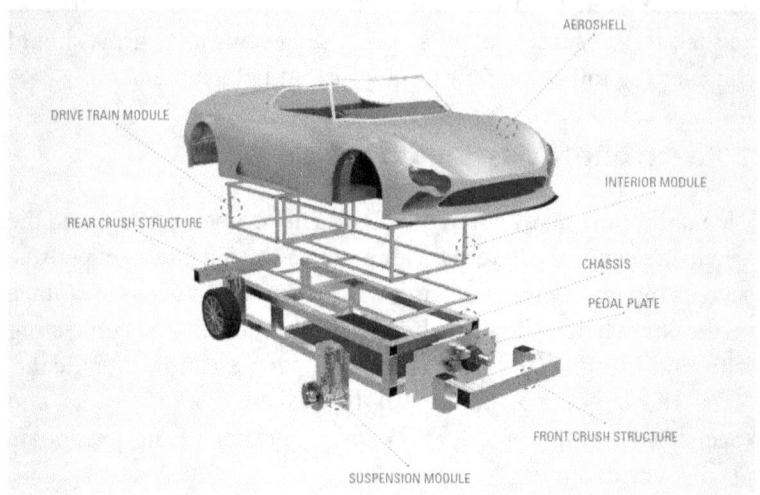

Wikispeed's Modular Architecture - Courtesy Joe Justice

4. Create opportunities for hands-on learning

At Wikispeed, continuous learning is encouraged and planned. Volunteers work in **pairings** of inexperienced and experienced individuals who take on small projects, and skills are quickly and mutually transmitted between team members. Volunteers work as much as possible on different modules so they acquire **skills** on the entire car.

Detroit Auto Show

In January 2011, Team Wikispeed received one of those offers one cannot refuse: they were invited to participate free of charge at the most famous car show in the world, the Detroit Auto Show. All of the most important car brands on the planet would be present. The team members were extremely excited but also literally terrified by the opportunity they were offered. Wikispeed's body used for the competition nicknamed the "orange shoe box," was not up to the task. It was necessary to design something more attractive for an international auto show. The team contacted some distributors of composite materials. Still, estimates and conditions were desolating – they would need 36,000 USD and three months to get the desired results, but there was no time or money. What to do?

Once again, the connection was decisive. A design-specialized Wikispeed-enthusiast technician spent various sleepless nights creating the design and sent his CAD project for a new body shell from Germany, which was later called the "Le Mans Version." In this case, nobody had ever met the author of a contribution that proved to be decisive.

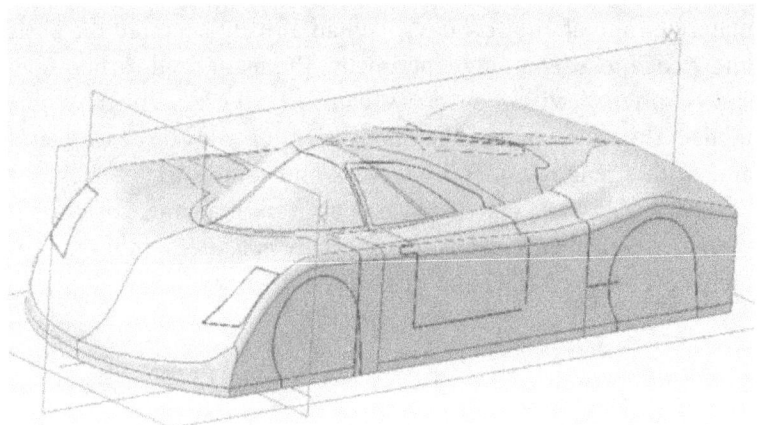

CAD of Le Mans version - Courtesy Joe Justice

In Joe's garage, volunteers began modeling the body shell with pressurized foam, first on a reduced scale, and then, with the aid of a CNC machine, they generated a real-size 3D model.

Body Shell Model - Courtesy Joe Justice

Joe took days off from work to attend a course on composite materials, and after a few days, he had already acquired the basic knowledge to attempt an experiment. The team used carbon fiber sheets softened with a special solvent to adhere perfectly to the model. They then painted the body shell of a lovely "race black" and, with strenuous smoothing work and some stickers, the most beautiful Wikispeed that had ever been seen came into existence. It was an incredible achievement, especially considering that the car body cost only 800 USD and three days of work.

Painting Work - Courtesy Joe Justice

Transport of the New Wikispeed Body - Courtesy Joe Justice

The fact that Wikispeed, in addition to offering outstanding performance, was also beautiful was, in turn, a decisive factor because, with great team surprise, the car was placed on the show's main floor, right in the middle between Ford and Chevrolet.

2011 Detroit Auto Show - Courtesy Joe Justice

Joe was still frightened by that environment – he expected to be snubbed by the other booths' white collars. Instead, one by one, the managers of each automobile company shook hands complimented him, and many wished him to start a real automobile company of his own. Joe was astonished: why did his competitors encourage him?

Subsequently, Joe stated in an interview that, in his view, the managers of the big companies were frustrated by the slowness with which things changed in larger companies and hoped that a new, small, aggressive, and ecological competitor would put the proper pressure needed to generate a fundamental change in their organizations. According to Joe, this explained his warm welcome that day.

Again, media coverage was massive. Wikispeed was mentioned by prominent newspapers such as Wired, National Geographic, New York Times Online, Forbes, and many specialized blogs, including Autoblog[172].

---

[172]http://www.autoblog.com/2011/01/12/detroit-2011-wikispeed-sgt01-low-cost-super-mpg-car/

Agile Alliance 2012

In 2012, the Wikispeed Team was well known on the international Agile scene, and Joe was invited as a keynote speaker to one of the most prestigious Agile conferences in the world: Agile 2012 of Agile Alliance[173] in Dallas, Texas.

2012 Agile Alliance - Courtesy Joe Justice

At the end of his speech, a participant asked a question to Joe:

> Joe, do you see Wikispeed manufacturing becoming a large-scale manufacturer?

His answer explains why, at the same time, he changed his profession and, from a software developer, he became Agile Coach:

> About 76 million new cars were built and sold last year. Current analysts predict that about that same number will be made again this year. We think at least 60 million of those should get 100 miles per gallon. That said, I don't want to figure out how to do the economies of

---

[173]https://www.agilealliance.org/resources/videos/keynote-joe-justice/

scale on 60 million cars manufactured in a year.

Even worse than that, I don't want to see the news that some manufacturing plant was shut down and 4,000 people in a neighborhood were laid off at once because they've just been put out of business by Wikispeed. I want Wikispeed to succeed.

I want it to grow in hundreds of thousands of cars a year because that's the number that will make an appreciable difference in the amount of fuel consumed and the number of emissions emitted. We could sell ten of these at 100,000 USD each, and my pocketbook would be pretty happy, or we could sell 100,000 of these at almost cost and make a difference for the environment. That's much more what I'm interested in.

Joe was only interested in creating a positive impact on the planet. He began to understand that teaching others to do likewise, according to the Wikispeed model, was the best way to boost its impact in less time. From that point, Wikispeed's focus moved to advocacy more than building cars.

Extreme Manufacturing Explained

Extreme Manufacturing is a set of principles created by Joe Justice during the WIKISPEED project. Those principles have been published by Peter Stevens[174], a Certified Scrum Trainer who lives in Zurich, Switzerland.

This chapter contains a copy of the original article Extreme Manufacturing Explained[175] enriched with photos, links, lexicon improvements, and additional notes.

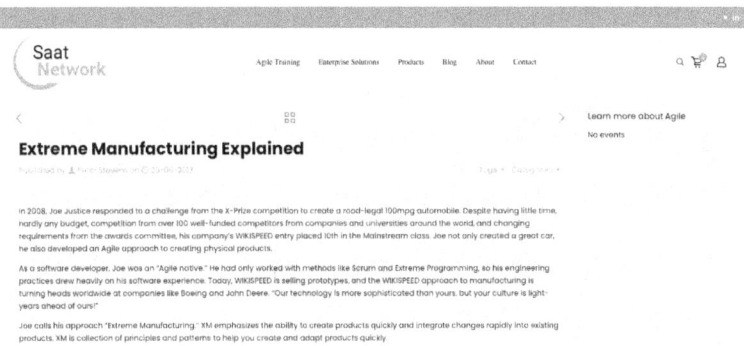

In 2008, Joe Justice responded to a challenge from the X-Prize competition to create a road-legal 100mpg automobile. Despite having little time, hardly any budget, competition from over 100 well-funded competitors from companies and universities worldwide, and changing requirements from the awards committee, his company's WIKISPEED entry placed 10th in the Mainstream class. Joe not only created a great car, but he also developed an Agile approach to creating physical products.

As a software developer, Joe was an "Agile native." He had only worked with Scrum and Extreme Programming methods, so his engineering practices drew heavily on his software experience. Today, WIKISPEED is selling prototypes, and the WIKISPEED approach

---

[174]https://saat-network.ch/about-saat-network/about-peter-stevens-cst/
[175]http://www.scrum-breakfast.com/2013/06/extreme-manufacturing-explained.html

to manufacturing is turning heads worldwide at companies like Boeing and John Deere. "Our technology is more sophisticated than yours, but your culture is light-years ahead of ours!"

Joe calls his approach "Extreme Manufacturing." XM emphasizes the ability to create products quickly and integrate changes rapidly into existing products. XM is a collection of principles and patterns to help you create and adapt products rapidly.

The list of the principles is the following:

1. Optimize for change
2. Object-Oriented, Modular Architecture
3. Test Driven Development
4. Contract-First Design
5. Iterate the Design
6. Agile Hardware Design Patterns
7. Continuous Integration Development
8. Continuously Deployed Development
9. Scaling Patterns
10. Partner Patterns

These principles and patterns do not represent the final wisdom on Agile manufacturing but rather a work-in-progress on the discovery of better ways to manufacture things.

1. Optimize for change

What happens if an engineer comes up with a way to build a safer car door? Can that new door be deployed right away? No. A stamping machine and a custom-made die produce that door. Together, they cost over 10 million US dollars and must first be amortized before the new door can be economically produced. Given the high costs, it can take ten years or more before that better door can enter production. You can see the impact of the need to amortize considerable investments in the slow, incremental changes in automobiles from year to year, even from decade to decade!

WIKISPEED can change its design every seven days. They employ tools like value stream mapping not merely to reduce the variance of products produced or to optimize the flow through the production line but also to reduce the cost of change. It does not cost them more to use a new design than an existing one. So, if they have a safer way to build the door today, they start using it next week.

"Welcoming and responding to change" represents core Agile values and principles (see the Agile Manifesto and the Principles behind the Agile Manifesto). So, by adopting this principle, you take a massive step towards becoming an Agile organization.

2. Object-Oriented, Modular Architecture

In the software industry until the 1980s, programs were developed on a procedural model. These procedural programming languages led to highly complex, unmaintainable solutions. A change to one part of the program usually requires changes throughout the program.

"Tightly coupled" architectures are still pervasive in automotive designs. A change to the suspension requires a change to the chassis, which requires a change to something else, which eventually impacts the entire car's design.

Today, software developers use "information hiding" and object-oriented design patterns to create loosely coupled, highly modular solutions. So you can change, for instance, the login process without having to modify other parts of your system.

At the X-Prize competition, many of the competitors dropped out. Why? As it became clear that there would be many entrants, the organizers planned to hold a race on city streets to determine the overall winner. This requirement was changed to a coast-to-coast rally, and finally, they settled on a race over a very demanding, closed-course racetrack. Each acceptance scenario posted very different demands on the suspension. These changes posed enormous challenges for teams that could not embrace change rapidly.

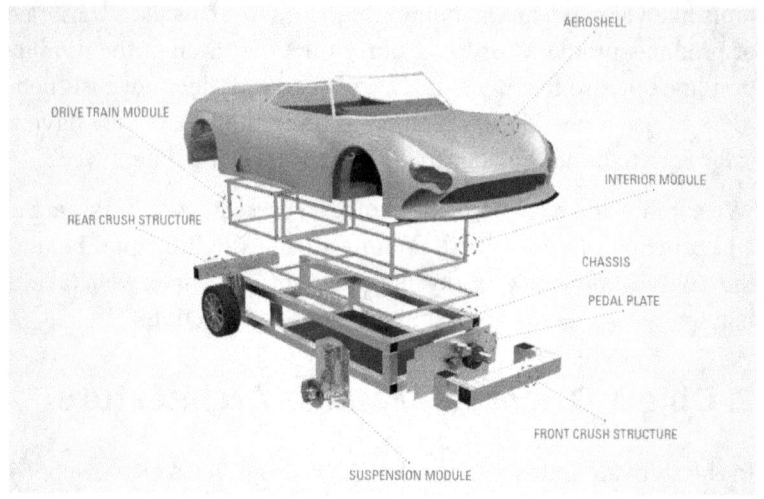

Wikispeed Modules - Courtesy Joe Justice

The WIKISPEED car is designed as eight modules, with simple interfaces between the modules. Due to its modular architecture, WIKISPEED was able to switch suspension systems with a minimum of fuss. WIKISPEED has also discovered it can apply related patterns, like inheritance and code reuse, to its advantage.

Embracing change is a core agile value. The ability to adapt rapidly meant WIKISPEED did better in the X-Prize competition than the nearly 100 entrants who dropped out without producing a car.

How do you achieve an object-oriented, modular architecture? The next two principles, 3 - Test-Driven Development and 4 - Contract-first Design, will help you.

3. Test-Driven Development

Before Joe started building a car, he created a model for predicting fuel economy. He identified over 100 well-known, freely available parameters, like weight, drag coefficients, engine power, tire size, etc. Based on these parameters, he could predict the car's EPA fuel economy within a few percent.

Armed with this model, he was able to calculate the characteristics the WIKISPEED entrant must have to achieve 100 miles per gallon and achieve performance characteristics worthy of a high-end sports car.

Team WIKISPEED wanted to achieve five-star crashworthiness according to the specifications of the NHTSA and IIHS. These specify impacts under multiple conditions to evaluate the crashworthiness of the cars. These tests are pretty expensive, US$10'000 per test, plus the costs of the vehicle itself, transport and disposal of the test vehicle, and the travel costs for the people involved. How can they update their designs every week when each change requires retesting? Step one was to use Finite Element Analysis to simulate the crashes. They ran an actual trial when they believed their car would pass the test.

Wikispeed Lateral Crash Test - Courtesy Joe Justice

Of course, they did not pass the test, but that was not the purpose. The Wikispeed team just wanted real crash data so they could better model crashes in their simulations. They updated their simulations based on the actual crash data. After a few iterations, their simulations became so good that the authorities now accept the results of their simulations in place of physical tests. Since they can now do (almost) fully automated tests, they can simulate crash tests every week.

When designing new components,

1. Create the test it is expected to pass. That can be very high level, like emissions tests or crash standards, or more component level. If it is possible to automate the test (or create an automated proxy for the test), do so, reducing the cost of repeating the test after future design changes.
2. Create the most uncomplicated design possible that enables the test to pass.
3. Iterate on the design, improving it until it is more valuable to work on another product portion.

In software, this process is known as "Red-Green-Refactor." To implement something, first create a test, which by definition fails immediately ("goes red"). Then implement functionality to make it pass (go green). Then improve the design for better maintainability, efficiency, etc. This is called refactoring.

4. Contract First Design

The initial design decision of the WIKISPEED car was that it should consist of eight modules – body, chassis, motor, suspension, interior, etc. Before Team WIKISPEED even started to design individual components, they developed the interfaces between those modules.

Joe did not know what suspension would be used on his car, but he could identify the external parameters and boundary conditions of the suspension. After researching the subject, he found that if the suspension mounting could withstand 8 gees, it would more than meet all the necessary requirements, even for Formula One racing applications. So the team identified a suitably sized block of aluminum that could carry that load. Any suspension attached to that block could be used on the WIKISPEED car without modification to the rest of the vehicle.

Wikispeed Suspension - Courtesy Joe Justice

So when designing a solution,

- Design the interfaces based on outside parameters, e.g., load factors or communication and power requirements.
- Only architect the connections up front, not the individual components.
- Leave room to grow, i.e., over-engineer these interfaces, because changing these fundamental contracts may be expensive.

P.S. Be sure to check out the Wrapper pattern to ensure independence between your design and the design of any component suppliers.

5. Iterate the Design

One frequently asked question for hardware or embedded projects considering Scrum is, "How can we get stuff done every sprint? It takes longer to develop a piece of hardware than could ever fit in a two-week sprint!" Hardware development needs to take a slightly different view on iterations than software development.

When the WIKISPEED engineers were first working on the interior, they realized that the lack of an emergency brake was slowing down their progress. The brake handle sits between the seats, close to the gearshift, and to the seats and seat belts attach points. Because no one knew what the emergency brake handle looked like, they were unwilling to decide on these nearby components.

The solution was "version 0.01" of the emergency brake: a cardboard box that said, "The brake handle will fit in this box." That was enough functionality so the team could move forward on nearby components, even though nobody had any illusions that this cardboard box would hold the car in place!

When working with hardware, you will iterate on your designs:

1. Create the test that your design should pass.
2. Create the most uncomplicated design possible that enables the test to pass.
3. Improve the design to be simpler or more elegant.
4. Repeat this process ("Iterate on the design") until improving this component is no longer your highest value work.

In the case of v0.01 of the emergency brake, the acceptance test was "Can the engineers design the surrounding components with confidence?" The cardboard box satisfied this test. Other components were judged to be of higher value, so they stayed with the cardboard box until the other parts were finished enough.

When developing software with Agile, each iteration should produce potentially deliverable functionality. That may not be possible when working with hardware, so you may need to iterate on a particular item many times before the design is satisfactory. In the case of the WIKISPEED X-Prize entrant, those subsequent iterations included, "An emergency brake to hold the car in place," and "An emergency brake which produces no resistance when the car is in motion."

You may also need to iterate on your acceptance tests, especially as you strive to automate them. Before WIKISPEED performed an actual crash test, they had done many Finite Element simulations. These are cheap and repeatable because all they need is computer time. Then they had a real crash test performed. That crash produced results that were different from their simulation, so they iterated. They used the real crash data to improve their simulation. Eventually, their simulations became close enough to reality that they no longer needed the expensive physical tests.

6. Agile Hardware Design Pattern

A pattern is an old idea. A design pattern is a simple way to represent implicit knowledge about well-known solutions to well-known problems. Patterns were pioneered in architecture by Christopher Alexander[176] to understand reasonable solutions to common challenges in building houses and other structures. Software developers picked up on the idea of communicating solutions to typical challenges in computer systems. WIKISPEED has identified many patterns to help suitable design hardware. For example:

1. Wrapper – Use a wrapper to adapt a third-party part to your contract. If you use the supplier's interface as your contractual interface, any product or supplier change will probably cause you to redesign the interface, a potentially expensive undertaking.
2. Facade – Use a façade, a connector of connectors with a simple interface, whenever multiple wires (like data & power) need to go to the same place.
3. Singleton – Every component needs power, data, and ground. Every engineer wants to create when designing a new part is

---

[176]https://wikipedia.org/wiki/Christopher_Alexander

the power, data, and ground bus. The singleton pattern says for each basis component, there is just one in use. So if you need a power-data-ground bus - use ours!

Sometimes the patterns have a cost. The wrapper pattern added 8 kg to the weight of a WIKISPEED car, for example, by adding an extra slab of aluminum between the chassis and the suspension.

Was the design pattern worth the extra weight? Yes, because that pattern allowed Team WIKISPEED to a) reduce several hundred pounds from the car's importance by continuous optimization and b) react quickly and cheaply to the changing suspension requirements. Had they not been able to do that, they would not have participated in the final selection round.

7. Continuous Integration Development

WIKISPEED has team members contributing in 20+ different countries, with variable availability any time of the day. How do they produce a cohesive, salient product? The answer has two parts. The first part is about engineering practices and the second about how to scale.

At the engineering level, Extreme Manufacturing employs Continuous Integration Development (CID) to run their test suite frequently (see principle 3 - Test Driven Development). Continuously Deployed Development (see principle 8) ensures a tight collaboration between product creation and product manufacturing, so the goal of never being more than 7 days from releasing an improved product can be achieved.

Continuous Integration Development (CID) ensures that the test suite is as automated as practical. Every time a team member sends in an updated design, an extensive test suite is run automatically.

Whenever a team member uploads a new 3d drawing to DropBox, Box.net, Windows SkyDrive, or any of the file-sharing technologies in use, WIKISPEED runs tests. WIKISPEED can simulate crash tests and stress tests on the part using FEA (Finite Element Analysis)[177] and a software package like LS Dyna[178] or AMPStech[179]. WIKISPEED can simulate airflow, aerodynamics, fluid flow, heat transfer, and electrical propagation using CFD (Computational Fluid Dynamics[180]).

Wikispeed simulated crash test - Courtesy Joe Justice

These tests can be run automatically whenever a new CAD shows up and write out a 1-page report with a list of red or green lights. Green lights mean the test is the same or better than the current version or passes an explicit test for that part or module.

In this way, team members worldwide can simultaneously contribute in parallel with very different ideas for improvements to each module. And it's easy to know the current best part; the version of record is whatever part in CAD has passed all tests with the most green lights.

---

[177]https://en.wikipedia.org/wiki/Finite_element_method
[178]https://en.wikipedia.org/wiki/LS-DYNA
[179]http://www.ampstech.com/
[180]https://en.wikipedia.org/wiki/Computational_fluid_dynamics

WIKISPEED includes tests for simplicity and low cost, along with user ergonomics, maintainability, manufacturability, and conformance to the interface(s) of the module they are a part of.

8. Continuously Deployed Development

Extreme Manufacturing requires going from an idea to a deliverable, working product, or service in 7 days or less. How do you produce a new design in volume in such a compressed timeline?

Let's look at how traditional companies address the problem of new product creation: When a conventional car manufacturer designs a new transmission, they build a new factory. Step one is to negotiate with various political districts for optimal conditions, e.g., access to roads & power, taxation requirements, etc. Then they acquire the land, build the facility, hire and train the workforce, and configure the line. After many years of preparation, their customers can finally order a product for delivery.

How do you compress years of lead time down to a one-week delivery cycle?

This Principle involves making the mass-manufacturing line flexible to produce different products within a 7-day sprint. These products might be existing, modified, or entirely new products.

Achieving this operational flexibility might mean additive or subtractive rapid prototyping machines or both. It might mean some devices or lean cells are placed on lockable casters so they can be wheeled in or out of the flow, depending on the sprint goal. This often means that the team reconfigures the machinery following daily Scrum each morning. And this invariably means test fixtures connected to andon lights[181] at all stages of the line.

R&D belongs at the head of the line. If the new product design team is within earshot of the volume manufacturing line, bi-directional

---
[181]https://en.wikipedia.org/wiki/Andon_(manufacturing)

communication occurs. If the R&D group deploys to the production line every sprint, both teams can work together to reconfigure the line to test and produce the new product. As cross-functional skill grows, any separation between the R&D and manufacturing teams dissolves, and we simply have the cross-functional product team. Each individual has specializations and welding certifications, but through pairing, they work on every aspect of the product flow from idea to customer delivery and support.

How will you get a genuinely marketable product if you only have seven days to create a new product? See XM Principle 5: Iterate the Design. The objective is to make the first version within a week. Then iterate on the design to improve it as needed. Use the intermediate results to get feedback from customers, users, and other stakeholders. Early designs will be big and clunky, using off-the-shelf components, but as you iterate the design and get feedback on it, you will zero in on your target.

For services, the story is precisely analogous. Ideally, the service providers are the advanced marketers and innovators of new services. Within a sprint, they interact with customers to improve the service and make the customers' improvements available.

9. Scaling Patterns

XM scales as Scrum scales, by adding teams. Coordination can occur through the Product Owners, Scrum Masters or Team Members, depending on the scope of the issues involved.

When multiple teams work on the same module, they each own a sub-module, which will require another finer pass of Contract-First Design to create interfaces for sub-modules before those teams can be made. For example, within the engine module, there is the fuel system module, the engine electronics module, the exhaust system module. Each module has an interface that loosely couples it with the other modules and explicit tests of their value and technical excellence.

Applied at WIKISPEED, the first design decision is the fundamental architecture of the product being created, in their case, a car. What are the main modules, e.g., engine, body, drive train, cockpit, etc., and what are the interfaces between them? Once the modules have been identified and the contacts between them created (see XM Principle 4: Contract-First Design), sub-teams can be made on each side of an interface to develop that module.

If capacity allows and velocity and quality metrics indicate that adding more teams per module will improve velocity and quality, multiple Scrum Teams can work in parallel per module.

Each team owns its own integration and tests. No team is "done" with an increment of their module until all tests pass, including tests that it complies with their module's interface, and no additional connections have been introduced.

Team Coordination

In XM Scrum of Scrums, teams consist of 4 to 5 people, including a Product Owner and Scrum Master. Each product owner is responsible for pulling stories from the Portfolio Product Backlog (or simply "Backlog") and clarifying when their team needs it on the customer's visible value and Net Present Value each story is intended to deliver.

This clarity comes from the Chief Product Owner (CPO), who continuously sequences and refines the Portfolio Product Backlog. The CPO is not a senior role in pay or experience but is the person available enough to keep backlog ready for the teams, answer questions, and have the most straightforward understanding of the customer visible value the Portfolio Product Backlog is aiming to produce. Ideally, the CPO is the customer and pays for the product or service the backlog seeks to create.

On each team, each Scrum Master is responsible for accelerating the team's velocity, i.e., the amount of work sustainably delivered each sprint. Sustainable implies that the teams are happy and that all work completed satisfies the quality metric called the Definition of Done. Scrum Masters have an additional job here: they collaborate with the Scrum Masters of other teams to negotiate the shared resources like space, tools, and modules across teams.

In this way, a team of 5 has clear expectations for themselves on how to resolve the most common types of impediments: lack of clarity is handled ASAP by the product owner, lack of backlog is dealt with ASAP by the product owner, lack of visibility into team delivery trend/quality/happiness is handled as a matter, of course, each week by the Scrum Master, and resource constraints and coordination are handled ASAP by the Scrum Master."

10. Partner Patterns

Deliveries often rely on third-party suppliers, and often they cannot deliver a new product that meets our new specifications within a single sprint. So what can we do to go from an idea to a new product or service in a customer's hands in less than 7 days?

WIKISPEED first designs a wrapper, usually a plate of aluminum with pre-defined bolt patterns. Around the third party supplied part to create a known "interface" that won't change, even if that third party part changes. You might see how this is enforced by principle 2: Object-Oriented, Modular Architecture and 4: Contract-First Design, and then sped up by principle 6: Agile Hardware Design Patterns.

Once each third-party part is wrapped in a known interface, you can iterate between suppliers and in-house prototypes or volume parts at a meager cost. The only marginal cost is that of changing the wrapper itself.

Then, to expedite suppliers, ask them to deliver a particular set of performance characteristics instead of an engineering specification. "Do you have a transmission suitable for a 100hp motor?" not "Here is our design for a transmission, can you build it?" Why should you wait months for a supplier to build a device to your specifications when they have a device that will satisfy your needs already in the catalog or in stock?

Many engineers are quick to design their own solution, which works to the team's advantage when the design team is also the volume manufacturing team. But in cases where some production is outsourced, sending a list of values and tests to the outsourced vendor and not sending an engineering specification gives the supplier the most room to innovate. This allows the vendor to do what they do best, that part, which is why you are partnering with them in the first place. Team WIKISPEED finds they get higher quality parts faster, often from within the vendor's existing stock.

Case Study Library

This chapter summarizes all the information about the case studies mentioned in the book's various parts.

Sisma Spa

Sisma[182] is an Italian company based in Piovene Rocchette (Vicenza, Italy). It was founded by Silvio Sbabo in 1961, has 220 employees, and has a turnover of over 55 million euros (2018).

The company manufactures high-precision machinery and laser systems with experience gained in over 130 machine models for the automatic production of gold chains.

Via dell'Industria 1
36013, Piovene Rocchette (VI)
Italia

info@sisma.com
www.sisma.com

The case study was presented for the first time on **September 14, 2019** at the "**Agile Business Day**" conference held at the

---

[182]https://www.sisma.com/en/corporate-sisma/

Department of Economics of the Ca'Foscari University in Venice. On stage with me, I had the pleasure to have **Vittorio Gaudino, CEO** of **Sisma Spa**.

The reference period of the story is between January 14, 2019, the kick-off of the transformation project, and June 25, 2019, the day of the Sprint Review number 7. The original video of the talk, Italian with English subtitles, is available on YouTube[183], while the slides can be downloaded on my personal website[184].

---

[183]https://youtu.be/-ytHed7iOaY
[184]https://paolo.sammiche.li/case-studies

Vimar Spa

Vimar[185] is an Italian company based in Marostica, Vicenza. Founded in 1945, in 2022, it has 1059 employees and a turnover of 274 million euros (Source: Wikipedia[186]). It owns over 180 patents and, with a catalog of 12,000 parts, has sold over 200 million pieces over the years. Traditionally, it produces electrical and electronic devices such as switches, sockets, video intercoms, alarm systems, thermostats, and civil and industrial components. Also, Vimar designs and sells smart devices with the most modern technologies. Today, with an investment in R&D of 6% turnover, Vimar ranks among the European leaders in the home automation solutions sector.

This case study was realized in collaboration with the company Festo CTE and published for the first time on **September 15, 2018**. It was presented during the conference "**Agile Business Day**" held at the Department of Economics of the University Ca'Foscari in Venice. On stage with me was **Giorgio Audisio**, R&D Director of Vimar Spa.

---

[185]https://www.vimar.com/
[186]https://it.wikipedia.org/wiki/Vimar

The reference period of the story is between January 16, 2017, the first day of LiftOff, and February 19, 2018, Sprint Review number 26. The original video of the talk, in Italian with English subtitles, is available on YouTube[187]. The slides can be downloaded on my personal website[188].

---

[187]https://youtu.be/gRckXtRq6ZI
[188]https://paolo.sammiche.li/case-studies

Pietro Fiorentini Spa

Pietro Fiorentini[189] is an international company that designs, produces, and installs equipment and complete solutions in the Oil and Gas sector, with over 80 years of history. It employs 1,700 people located in 13 plants: 6 in Italy and 7 in the rest of the world. The commercial offices cover Europe, Asia, America, and Africa.

This case study was published on **12 September 2020** during the "**Agile Business Day**" conference held online due to the Pandemic. I presented the story together with **Andrea Provaglio**, an independent Enterprise Coach and longtime friend who takes care of the company's Agile Transformation with me, and **Andrea Aganetti**, **Product Owner** of **Pietro Fiorentini Spa**.

The reference period is between 22 July 2019, the Kick-Off of the project described, and 20 November 2019, the day of the Sprint Review number 7. The original video of the talk is available on YouTube[190]. The slides can be downloaded from my personal website[191].

---

[189]https://www.fiorentini.com/en/

[190]https://www.youtube.com/watch?v=DXpFDFoZOC4

[191]https://paolo.sammiche.li/case-studies

Net Engineering

NET Engineering[192] is an independent Italian engineering and architecture company highly specialized in the design of transport infrastructure, urban redevelopment, and engineering design serving the industrial sector.

This case study was published with Silvia Furlan, Net Engineering CEO, on **8 July 2021** during the "**Agile Bim Meetup.**"

The reference period of the story is between January 2020 and July 2021. The original video of the talk is available on YouTube[193]. The slides can be downloaded on my personal website[194].

---

[192]https://www.net-italia.com/en/
[193]https://www.youtube.com/watch?v=-D5sfh9sals
[194]https://paolo.sammiche.li/case-studies

Appendix

As the Author
I want to have additional material
So that the reader gets more value with this book.

In this last part, you will find additional material about Business Agility that comes from my previous book "Scrum for Hardware," so that I can reference them without you having to necessarily read my other book.

Popcorn Flow

In this chapter, you find the interview with Claudio Perrone[195], author of Popcorn Flow[196], where he explains his method.

Hi Claudio, thanks for your time. Let's start with the most obvious question: What is PopcornFlow?

PopcornFlow is a method to introduce, sustain, and accelerate continuous innovation & change. It promotes ultra-rapid experimentation to make better decisions under uncertainty.

It consists of two parts: a decision cycle and a set of principles.

Most people come across PopcornFlow through its 7-step decision cycle. No surprises there, as the word *Popcorn* stands for the initials of each step:

---

[195]https://www.linkedin.com/in/claudioperrone/
[196]https://popcornflow.com/

- Problems and observations
- Options
- Possible experiments
- Committed
- Ongoing
- Review
- Next

Teams and individuals reason about the problems they face, options to neutralize or reduce the impact of those problems, and possible experiments to explore one or more of those options. Either just-in-time or on a fast cadence, they capture the details on sticky notes and place them on a PopcornFlow board - a visual board that represents each step as a column. They then *flow* experiments through the board, bringing to the surface (what I call) a *learning stream*. I often work with small teams where we co-design several experiments per week.

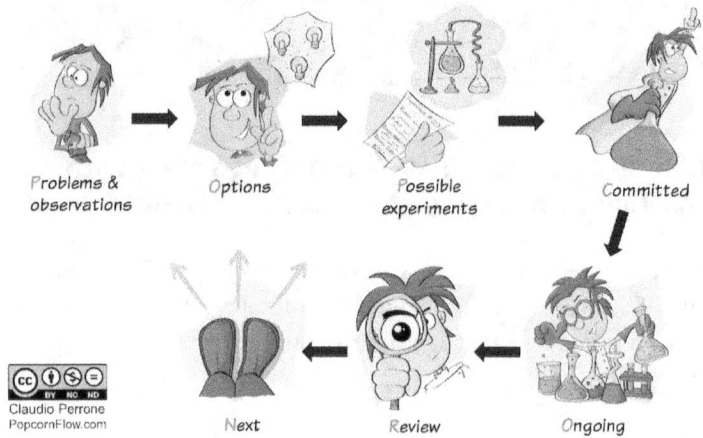

Claudio Perrone
PopcornFlow.com

The decision cycle reveals only part of the story - the machinery. The secret to unleashing PopcornFlow lies in its guiding principles:

1. If change is hard, make it continuous (The Virus Principle).

2. It's not only what you do but also what you learn by doing it that matters (The Ladder Principle).

3. Everybody is entitled to their own opinion, but a shared opinion is a fact (The Freedom Principle).

4. It's not "fail fast, fail often." It's "learn fast, learn often" (The Skateboarder Principle).

5. Small bets, big win. (Note: The wording of this last principle is still a work in progress, but it's based on Nassim Taleb's concept of "option asymmetry." In a nutshell, it's not about how frequently we meet or exceed our expectations. It's rather about how to limit the cost of each experiment and how much we gain when we are - even if occasionally - right.)

How was PopcornFlow born?

I love origin stories!

I struggled to come to terms with the debacle of my latest entrepreneurial adventure when Eric Ries took the startup world by storm. He observed that startups operate under extreme uncertainty conditions and promoted a sort-of scientific approach to validate assumptions and converge to a viable business model. The Lean Startup movement was born. Right away, I fiddled with those ideas, both for my own projects and for my clients - many of which were, in fact, fast-growing startups. As I needed to track experiments systematically, I created many Kanban board designs, which admittedly ranged from borderline simplistic to overly complex.

At a conference in Boston, however, something magical happened: Jeff Anderson[197] took the stage to show how he applied Lean Startup concepts to organizational change. He called this Lean Change[198], an approach that was later forked and popularized by Jason Little[199]. Jeff argued that people react to change is highly contextual and

[197]https://www.linkedin.com/in/thomasjeffreyandersontwin/
[198]https://leanpub.com/leanchangemethod
[199]https://leanchange.org/

unpredictable ways. As a result, a team of change agents involved in any large organizational transformation inevitably faces extreme uncertainty conditions - a situation analogous to a startup. Wow, that was a smashing realization! It was early days, and the session was hotly debated. I chatted with Jeff right afterward. Frankly, neither the scenario Jeff had described at the time - an appointed team of change agents experimenting *on* change recipients - nor most of the implementation details felt quite right. But it didn't matter: I realized I could devote my efforts and tools to co-design experiments and negotiate change *with* people in organizations.

I wasted no time. Back in Europe, a startup urged me to help them address a critical situation to their survival. Their (anything-but) Scrum development team had been unable to release software for months due to quality and integration problems. People were distributed across several countries. The most troubling aspect was that the company had outsourced core parts of the platform to a third-party company. Their management had since gone rogue: their lack of transparency and shady tactics had created an unsustainable situation.

With the motto "soft on people, hard on systems," we agreed to go back to basics and resume Scrum. My aim was to put a solid process in place, establish radical transparency, and treat with respect everyone involved in the production line - including the external partners.

I explained that Agile is not about ceremonies. It's about humility: we don't pretend to know and impose The One True Way to develop software. So, we start with what we know so far and then continuously inspect and adapt our approach. During our weekly retrospectives, we negotiated small change experiments to improve how we worked together. For example, in our communication, the tools we used, how we reviewed our code, and much more. We visually tracked problems and observations - facts but also very personal opinions. We acted on the ones we could agree with (or, at least, not violently disagree with). It was all there for people to see. And so, with little fanfare, PopcornFlow became a natural way to facilitate our Scrum retrospectives.

Every week, I asked these questions:

- What experiments did we agree to do?
- Which one did we actually do?
- What did we expect to happen?
- What did we learn?
- Based on what we learned, what are we going to do next?

Some experiments met our expectations. Others didn't. But as the co-designed experiments entered the cycle, the team's climate improved steadily. Little by little, people's confidence grew. They experimented several times throughout each Sprint. Even one improvement experiment each week would have been enough. Instead, they launched 5 or 6 of those every week - sometimes even 10! It didn't take long for the results to arrive. The company went from being unable to release the product for months to release it several times a day. My job was done.

I saw their PopcornFlow board once again, almost a year later. It had captured hundreds of experiments. Unsurprisingly, as the company grew, other boards had appeared in other parts of the organization, well outside the original development team. PopcornFlow had impacted marketing, sales, and strategy.

Then a friend of mine - an Agile coach who had introduced PopcornFlow in his organization - suggested: "Claudio, drop everything else and focus on PopcornFlow. This thing is freaking amazing."

So I did.

What makes PopcornFlow different?

Some practitioners have originally likened the PopcornFlow steps to PDCA/PDSA[200], the well-known Shewhart[201]/Deming[202] cycle. The similarity is only superficial, however. They operate in very different domains of complexity. Like two faces of the same coin, they are opposite and complementary.

With PDSA, we deliberately "go slow to go fast." With PopcornFlow, we "go fast to learn faster." The former is about *continuous improvement*, the latter is about *continuous change*. But above all, PDSA's approach is based on root-cause analysis and the scientific method, PopcornFlow is not! Consider the Freedom Principle I mentioned before, for example. (Don't worry: it has *metaphorical* rather than *literal* meaning.) Subjectivity plays a primary role, and we can exploit it. It doesn't sound very *scientific*, does it?

Over time, I developed a more refined sense of the forces at work and realized that PopcornFlow best operates in complex rather than complicated domains (see Dave Snowden's Cynefin[203] framework). In this context, PopcornFlow problems are, essentially, system *probes*. To a great extent, we use uncontrolled parallel experiments to *explore options* and change the system dynamics. In fact, I even came to question Lean Startup's scientific claims, particularly around the idea of *validated learning*. Is it possible that maybe we are doing the right things for the wrong reasons?

And so, despite its origins, PopcornFlow has changed and evolved into something different. Its decision cycle is, perhaps, a very pragmatic expression of John Boyd's OODA loop[204]; its philosophy echoes Nassim Taleb's Antifragile[205] approach.

---

[200]https://en.wikipedia.org/wiki/PDCA
[201]https://en.wikipedia.org/wiki/Walter_A._Shewhart
[202]https://en.wikipedia.org/wiki/W._Edwards_Deming
[203]https://en.wikipedia.org/wiki/Cynefin_framework
[204]https://en.wikipedia.org/wiki/OODA_loop
[205]https://en.wikipedia.org/wiki/Antifragile

In which areas have you seen people using PopcornFlow?

My observation is that organizations want to innovate, but they don't know how to do it. PopcornFlow is relatively young and still evolving. Yet, it already found its way in startups, large financial institutions, well-known technology companies, and more. Last year, a group in the Canadian public sector, for example, won two prestigious national innovation awards; the secret - they revealed - was *a magic trick up their sleeve.* I often use PopcornFlow to coach Agile teams and facilitate highly effective retrospectives. Teams trade options outside their immediate circle, too - a crucial mechanism to reduce the inevitable bias. Combined with jobs-to-be-done theory, it also works well for product and service innovation. I'm occasionally called to help sales and marketing teams too. Basically, if you need to introduce change, PopcornFlow may be a good fit. There is nothing intrinsically technological or "corporate" about it. I even use it to negotiate change with my kid (who is at the high-functioning end of the autism spectrum[206]). It's been used by families, job seekers, school teachers, life coaches, psychologists, and more. You see? It's about decisions. And life is full of those.

What can we expect from PopcornFlow in the future?

Workshops, coaching, and speaking gigs aside, these days, I'm developing a digital platform and writing a book. I am trying hard to keep the technical jargon to a minimum and, hopefully, reach a wider audience. I designed PopcornFlow to be *so simple that even a five-year-old child could understand it.* "This way," I thought, "grown-ups will understand it too." My son became quite proficient at that age, but the jury's still out on some adults. Ah ah.

Interview ©2018 Claudio Perrone, Paolo Sammicheli.

---

[206]https://www.autismspeaks.org/what-autism/asperger-syndrome

Cynefin

The complexity theory is a widely debated topic in various science branches, and there is no generally defined definition of what **complexity** is. Cynefin[207] is a decision-making framework developed by Dave Snowden within IBM in the early 2000s that provides a concise and straightforward management strategy for each of the domains defined. In addition to being used in IBM, Cynefin is applied to product development, market analysis, supply chain management, branding, customer relationship management, emergency management, and several other critical areas by the government of many countries worldwide. Now, let us examine the Cynefin Framework in greater detail.

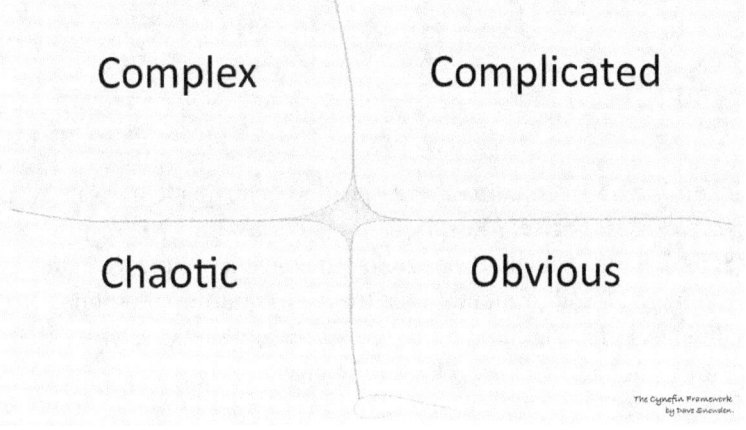

The Cynefin model has four domains (Obvious, Complicated, Complex, Chaotic), represented as four quadrants. It suggests a clear strategy. A fifth domain called Disorder and illustrated in the center

[207]https://en.wikipedia.org/wiki/Cynefin_framework

is a situation where there is no clarity about which of the other domains apply.

Obvious Domain

In the Obvious domain, components are strongly coupled. This is a predictable and understandable domain; knowledge is enough to deal with the issues involved in this spectrum.

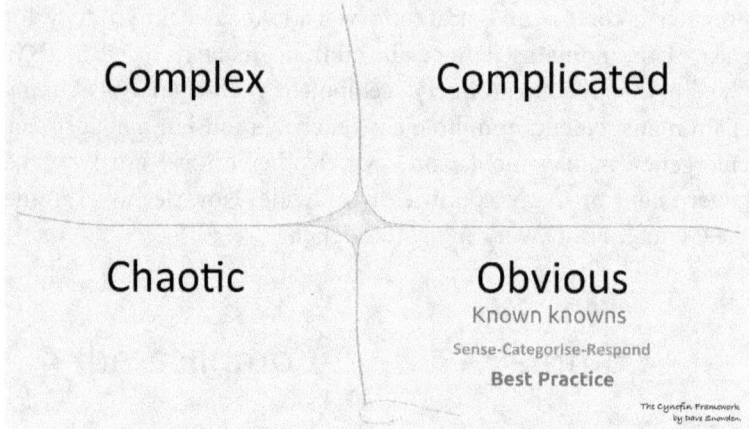

In an Obvious domain, the associated management strategy is **Sense - Categorise - Respond**. Considering the type of problem (Sense), we use our knowledge to recognize its reference category (Categorise) and respond with the best solution (Respond). An Obvious domain is characterized by the Best Practices, where there is only one optimal way to solve the problem.

Complicated Domain

In the Complicated domain, components are coupled by a cause-effect relationship, but this is not easily understandable. Our expertise is thus not sufficient to address the problem immediately as in the Obvious domains.

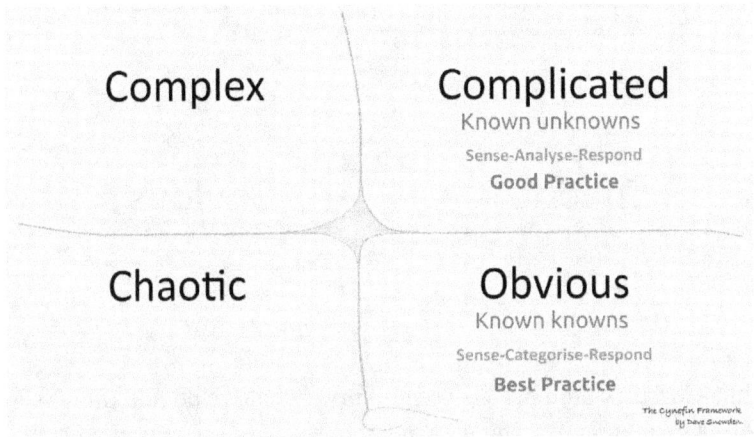

In a Complicated domain, the associated management strategy is **Sense – Analyse - Respond**. In other words, realizing the type of issue (Sense), we study it in detail (Analyse) and find the most appropriate response (Respond). A Complicated domain does not have a single optimal solution but several Good Practices. These different methods are equally worth that allows solving the problem effectively.

Complex Domain

In a Complex domain, interactions between different components are not clearly perceptible a priori.

In a Complex domain, we do not know what we do not know (Unknown Unknowns). The management strategy associated with this domain is **Probe - Sense - Respond**. This involves performing an experiment (Probe), observing the results (Sense), and responding accordingly (Respond), probably with a new investigation capable of expanding our knowledge. In this context, the approach is iterative and incremental, and practices are called Emergent Practices precisely because they emerge during the discovery process.

Chaotic Domain

In the Chaotic domain, it is impossible to know what we do not know (Unknowable Unknowns). An experiment repeated infinitely in a Chaotic domain always produces different results, so it is useless. Studying a Chaotic domain is even more useless.

The management strategy in a Chaotic domain is **Act - Sense - Respond**. In practice, we need to act (Act), understand what happens while we act (Sense), and try to respond quickly (Respond). Fortunately, a Chaotic domain in nature persists for a short time and tends to stabilize towards a Complex domain.

Disorder

When we do not know the domain we are in, the Cynefin model calls it Disorder. It is represented by the dark area in the center of the diagram. In this area, the belonging domain is by definition challenging to understand. According to Snowden, the way out of this domain is to break down the situation into constituent parts and assign each of the other four domains previously mentioned.

Conclusions

Cynefin provides a contextual approach advantageous to managers to orient themselves in the growing complexity of today's challenges.

This is a significant change from a cultural perspective. Instead of obsessively trying to predict the future by understanding it, the management must have iterative and incremental processes that allow safe-to-fail experiments that can incorporate learning gained in successive strategic choices.

Further readings

- A Leader's Framework for Decision Making[208] - Dave Snowden, Mary E. Boone
- Cynefin - Weaving Sense-Making into the Fabric of Our World[209] - Dave Snowden, Zhen Goh

---

[208]https://hbr.org/2007/11/a-leaders-framework-for-decision-making
[209]https://www.goodreads.com/book/show/55813487-cynefin---weaving-sense-making-into-the-fabric-of-our-world

Agile Management

An Agile Manager does not do a different job than a traditional manager: like all managers, he *takes difficult decisions*. The difference lies in the way he does it. An Agile Manager has understood and metabolized the concept of complexity, as defined in the Cynefin model, previously described here in the appendix. He needs to "knows not to know." Peter Stevens[210] once told me, "**complicated** is when I know the questions but not the answers, **complex** is when I do not even know the questions". An Agile Manager makes decisions by prioritizing the ability to cope with change. He knows that nothing is definitive, which is why he explores, with the rest of the organization, a world that is a continuous discovery. Agile is a management style closer to the definition of Leadership, and acquiring it requires going through a long and winding path. A list of practical suggestions can be found in the Management 3.0[211] material by Jurgen Appelo[212], of which I reproduce here a small extract.

Guidelines for Managers in Complexity

1. Address complexity with complexity
2. Use a diversity of perspectives
3. Assume subjectivity and coevolution
4. Steal and tweak
5. Assume dependence on context
6. Anticipate, adapt, explore
7. Reduce the feedback cycle
8. Keep options open

---

[210]https://www.scrumalliance.org/community/profile/pstevens
[211]https://management30.com/
[212]http://jurgenappelo.com

Address complexity with complexity

The most complex tool available to you is your brain. To make sense of complex problems, you can use storytelling, metaphors, and visualization tools. **A system's complexity must be adjusted to the complexity of the system it is in**, says Michael R. Lissack in the book "The Interaction of Complexity and Management[213]"

Use a diversity of perspectives

Complexity per se is an anti-methodology, as opposed to the concept of the silver bullet, functional in every context, which instead the methodologies tend to propose.

Combining a set of different perspectives, even if not perfectly positioned, produces a better point of view than a single well-defined point of view. This is the purpose, for example, of the collaboration between the Product Owner, who has a business focus, with the Development Team, which has a technical focus, in the Scrum Team itself with a single objective.

Assume subjectivity and coevolution

Complex systems are often also adaptive: their complexity is intrinsic and due to a natural and unpredictable evolution of the system. In this context, the observer influences the observed system, just as the system, in turn, affects the observer. When cause and effect are interdependent, one can solve a situation even by focusing on another.

Steal and tweak

Successful systems spend much of their time copying and adapting ideas from others. Innovation is often imagined as a process of

---

[213]https://www.goodreads.com/book/show/4852736-the-interaction-of-complexity-and-management

creating new things from scratch; usually, however, invention passes from the transposition of a good idea from one domain to another or from an unprecedented combination of existing ideas.

Assume dependence on context

Be skeptical: it is not sure that what worked in the past or for other functions will work today for you too. "Any relationship that anyone identifies between a management action and an obtained result may have more to do with time and place than with the action itself," says Ralph Stacey, for example in the book "Complexity and Organizational Reality[214]".

Anticipate, adapt, explore

Explore a situation by imagining improvements (anticipate), trying something (explore), and responding to the change you get (adapt). In the book "The Toyota Way[215]" we read, in fact, "An evolving and improving system requires by its nature a continuous experimentation".

Reduce the feedback cycle

"The only way to win is to learn faster than others," says Eric Ries in the book "The Lean Startup[216]". Systems that have a slower feedback loop have a higher extinction rate. It is necessary to iterate every day faster and faster.

Keep options open

In the book The Interaction of Complexity and Management[217], we read, "The absorption of complexity involves creating risk hedging

---

[214]https://www.goodreads.com/book/show/9927574-complexity-and-organizational-reality
[215]https://www.goodreads.com/book/show/161789.The_Toyota_Way
[216]https://www.goodreads.com/book/show/10127019-the-lean-startup
[217]https://www.goodreads.com/book/show/4852736-the-interaction-of-complexity-and-management

options and strategies", even outside your expectations. Get ready for any kind of surprise.

In Detail

Another aspect to take into consideration is the ability of systems theory[218]. We need to make decisions that involve and consider the whole system to avoid actions that locally appear to be good but that do not improve, or in the worst cases, degrade the performance at the system level. Peter Senge extensively explores this theme, for example, in the book "The fifth discipline[219]".

Further readings

Agile management's topic is extensive, and a complete discussion is beyond the scope of this book. Those who wish to further explore the subject are advised to read the following:

- The Leader's Guide to Radical Management: Reinventing the Workplace for the 21st Century[220] - Stephen Denning
- The Fifth Discipline: The Art & Practice of The Learning Organization[221] - Peter Senge
- Management 3.0: Leading Agile Developers, Developing Agile Leaders[222] - Jurgen Appelo
- The Interaction of Complexity and Management[223] - Michael Lissack
- Complexity and Organizational Reality[224] - Ralph D. Stacey

---

[218]https://en.wikipedia.org/wiki/Systems_theory

[219]https://en.wikipedia.org/wiki/The_Fifth_Discipline

[220]https://www.goodreads.com/book/show/8873049-the-leader-s-guide-to-radical-management

[221]https://www.goodreads.com/book/show/255127.The_Fifth_Discipline

[222]https://www.goodreads.com/book/show/10210821-management-3-0

[223]https://www.goodreads.com/book/show/4852736-the-interaction-of-complexity-and-management

[224]https://www.goodreads.com/book/show/9927574-complexity-and-organizational-reality

How to interview the Scrum Master

The selection of the Scrum Master is not defined anywhere in the Scrum Guide. Who chooses him? With which criteria?

Different methods can be observed: in some cases, the Scrum Master offers voluntarily and is then appointed by the management; in others, he was born as a member of the Team and is elected within it, and often partly continues to carry out development activities, as a team member.

At the beginning of 2018, one of my clients needed to reorganize the development department to harmonize his teams. His Scrum Masters, elected among the team members, carried out their part-time role and continued to work on development as well. Various problems were emerging: in some teams, there was an overabundance of aspiring Scrum Masters while in others, the role had been played by the person with more seniority of service, without however manifesting a great enthusiasm. Playing a role partially also reduced the focus. It provided an alibi for not devoting time to the study of coaching practices.

I suggested taking advantage of the reorganization to experiment with a different method of choosing the Scrum Master, taking inspiration from Craig Larman's LeSS method.

Considering the existing constraint, which required maintaining the number of people employed (*headcount*), Scrum Master would become a full-time assignment. Each Scrum Master would be assigned to two teams. Those wishing to become Scrum Masters should apply to an internal Job Posting and pass an assessment interview held by the Coaches who led the transformation. After that, the teams would indicate their preferences among the selected people. The management would finalize the pairings, trying to satisfy as many people as possible.

The idea of having full-time and professionalized Scrum Masters convinced everyone in the company, and the managers decided to experiment with this different method. The top management assured me that Scrum Master would be a role and not a *job title*. With the mantra "Job and Salary safety, Role unsafety," the new organization was announced to the whole company development department.

Selection Criteria

I began to think about what could be the way to select candidates. Scrolling back to the book by Lyssa Atkins "Coaching Agile Teams"[225] I pondered on the multiplicity of roles that the Agile Coach must play, and in particular on its three main functions:

- Trainer
- Facilitator
- Coach

I also had a look at "Succeeding with Agile" by Mike Cohn[226] with his acronym *ADAPT*, which is about Awareness, Desire, Ability, Practice, and Transfer. I had a crazy intuition: if ADAPT works for organizations, why shouldn't it be suitable for an individual?

Therefore, I tried to place the meaning of each letter within the context of an aspiring Scrum Master:

- Awareness of the role, and of oneself.

---

[225]https://www.goodreads.com/book/show/8337919-coaching-agile-teams
[226]https://www.goodreads.com/book/show/6707987-succeeding-with-agile

- Desire of the role and how they see themselves into the role.
- Ability to read coaching situations.
- Practice. The practical skills as a facilitator.
- Transfer. The ability to transfer concepts, to teach.

This skill *checklist* seemed to cover well the roles of trainer, facilitator, and coach of the book "Coaching Agile Teams"[227].

The Interview

The interview was held in a dedicated room. With the candidates' permission, it was audio recorded so that the interviewer would not need to take notes during the interview and focus on the candidate.

The **Awareness** component was explored with two questions:

1. What characteristics should a Scrum Master have?
2. What characteristics, among those you have listed, do you think you have, and on which do you think you have to work harder?

For question 1, there were correct and well-documented answers even in the Certified Scrum Master courses, question 2 aimed at understanding how people were aware of the personal growth path required by the role.

For the **Desire** part, the questions were:

3. Why do you want to be a Scrum Master?
4. Think about yourself tomorrow. You are a Scrum Master. What has changed in you, and what do others say about you?

---

[227]https://www.goodreads.com/book/show/8337919-coaching-agile-teams

Question 3 aimed at understanding if the motivation was related to the role, career, and prestige or if it also derived from the presence of soft relational skills, perhaps developed outside of the working context, with hobbies, sports, and voluntary activities. Question 4 sought to explore how the candidates saw themselves in the role; any awareness of the difficulties would be considered favorably.

The **Ability** part was conducted with two situational questions:

5. In a team of four developers, one person always does solo work. Others suffer from this but do not openly say anything. You are their Scrum Master. What will you do?

6. A manager who has not fully understood Scrum enters the team room and complains that a feature he had promised a client has not been completed yet. The relative story has dragged for a further 2 sprints beyond what expected. He alludes to the fact that the Team does not commit itself. You are the Scrum Master, and you are in the room at that moment. What will you do?

These questions evaluated compliance with the Scrum Guide's principles, the quantity, and quality of options that people listed. An approach in line with systemic thinking and complexity, described in in the Appendix, paragraphs Agile Management and Cynefin.

The **Practice** component aimed at evaluating facilitation and visualization capabilities. The candidate was asked to visualize on a flip chart the concepts that were read from a book[228] as if they were dialogues that emerged in a meeting. Like in discussions, the facilitator can intervene to ask a question but cannot monopolize the speech. It was then explained to the candidate that it was not dictation but a way to visualize the key concepts and that they could interrupt the reading by asking questions without exaggerating.

---

[228]In the case described here, I read to the candidates the chapter "The Fourth Industrial Revolution" from my first book "Scrum for Hardware" https://leanpub.com/Scrum-for-Hardware

This test aimed at evaluating the writing, the order, and the use of color.

Finally, for the **Transfer** part, it was asked to explain what Agile was in the first question and how Scrum worked in a second one. The candidate could use the flip chart if he thought it helpful. The questions were always asked in a situational way (e.g., I am a consultant for a foreign branch, I am traveling in development and meeting you. I invite you to explain what Agile means, the term I heard at a meeting the same morning). Moreover, it was assessed how much the answer strove to adapt to the context and vocabulary of the person who posed the question in the imagined situation.

Evaluation

The evaluation of the candidates' responses was carried out later, listening to the audio recordings and analyzing the photos of the artifacts produced in the Practice and Transfer questions. At first, the critical aspects of the answers were noted. A grade was then assigned on a scale similar to the Italian scholar one, from 4 to 8. A second evaluation tried to harmonize the judgments once all the interviews were listened to have a balanced vote between the candidates. A summary table was then created in which there was a single vote for each individual component of ADAPT. However, the individual grades were not added to get the final ranking; instead, to try to absorb the complexity of the choice of a suitable Scrum Master, those with serious fails were first discarded. Then, the remaining ones were ordered case by case, trying to evaluate the candidate in its entirety and not based on the mere algebraic sum of votes. The goal was to build a list of ordered people to enter the role to select those who had the smallest gap to fill.

Outcomes

The development department involved in the process had about 100 employees distributed between systems engineers, support groups, and 10 Scrum teams. The goal was to identify 5 Scrum Master candidates.

As stated to the management before starting the interviews, I would consider this process a success if it surprised me. I other words, if the suitable people emerged from it who had not already seemed such since the beginning of the Agile transition. Of the 5 new Scrum Masters selected, two were former developers. They had managed to overcome in the rankings people who acted as Scrum Masters for about two years, despite not having held this role previously. This showed how much potential and hidden talent there were in them. However, many people excluded from the final choice had demonstrated that they had characteristics of suitability, and this was reassuring in the possible future prospect of having to repeat the process for an enlargement of the workforce or in case of refusals. The new Scrum Masters all showed great enthusiasm, and the first feedback after some Sprints are very encouraging. At the time of the writing of this book, beginning of 2021 - three years after the first use of this practice, I used this approach multiple times in different companies, with a total of nearly thirty candidates. I consider this a valuable tool that helped me to identify suitable candidates for the role in several companies. In particular, three times, my assessment showed a not suitability for candidates. Still, they got employed anyway. In all the cases, they showed significant difficulties in entering the role and progressing with the learning.

Electronic Version

To download the electronic version of this book, follow this link or scan the QRCode:

https://leanpub.com/scrum-hardware-explained/c/carta

The link will work up to 31 December 2027.

Previous Version free access

To download "**Scrum for Hardware**," the previous book on this topic, in a DRM-Free PDF and EPUB format, follow this link or scan the QRCode:

https://leanpub.com/Scrum-for-Hardware/c/new23

The link will work up to 31 December 2028.

This page intentionally left blank

www.ingramcontent.com/pod-product-compliance
Lightning Source LLC
Chambersburg PA
CBHW070619220526
45466CB00001B/64

9 798397 938815